Su
MCL 9/12

COMPLETE SURRENDER

COMPLETE SURRENDER

DAVE SHARP AND JOHN PARKER

WITH A FOREWORD BY

IAN McEWAN

THE TRUE STORY OF A FAMILY'S
DARK SECRET AND THE BROTHERS
IT TORE APART AT BIRTH

JOHN BLAKE

First published in hardback in 2008

ISBN: 978 1 84454 582 7

British Library Cataloguing-in-Publication Data:

A catalogue record for this book is available from the British Library.

Design by www.envydesign.co.uk

Printed in UK by CPI William Clowes, Beccles, NR34 7TL

1 3 5 7 9 10 8 6 4 2

Papers used by John Blake Publishing are natural, recyclable products made from wood grown in sustainable forests. The manufacturing processes conform to the environmental regulations of the country of origin.

Every attempt has been made to contact the relevant copyright-holders, but some were unobtainable. We would be grateful if the appropriate people could contact us.

For Oliver and Benjamin

ACKNOWLEDGEMENTS

When I suggested to my brother that my experiences would make a good story, and he had replied, 'no it's your story, you write it', I had no idea how much help and goodwill I would need from so many people to turn my pages of words into a book. To say 'thanks' to everyone who has helped me doesn't seem adequate, but here goes and if I do miss someone out I hope they won't cross me off their Christmas card list.

To Lieutenant Colonel (Retired) Colin Fairclough of the Salvation Army Family Tracing Service for his diligence and professional approach to his work.

To John Parker for his friendship and for helping me to unjumble my story and give it readability.

To my brother Ian for his support and for taking the time to write a truly great foreword for my book.

My agent Sheila Ableman for her help and advice.

John Shotton, a former friend and fellow officer of

my father, for allowing me to use extracts of letters he had written.

To Daniel Bunyard, senior editor at John Blake Publishing, for his continued guidance.

Finally, but by no means least, to Julie, for her unlimited support and boundless patience with me.

CONTENTS

'When my father and mother forsake me, then the Lord will take me up.'

Psalm 27, verse 10

READING STATION

A FOREWORD BY IAN MCEWAN

In the winter of 1942, a pretty woman in her mid twenties holding her six-week-old baby boarded a train at the Victorian garrison town of Aldershot; travelling with her was her younger sister carrying a bundle of the baby's clothing. Their plan was simple and momentous, as well as illegal. They would travel half an hour or so to the town of Reading and there on the platform, as arranged, give the child away, along with a falsely made-out birth certificate, to a man and woman, total strangers. We know that the sisters, overwhelmed by grief, returned straight home. At this remove, moral judgements are irrelevant. The young mother was attempting to resolve what must have seemed an intractable problem and, in the most limited terms, she succeeded: nothing was heard from this baby boy for another sixty years.

Her name was Rose Wort, and the son she abandoned to

his fate is my older brother, David, whose story this is. To understand fully this singular, painful event would require the resources of an omniscient god. The full story is beyond our reach. In that moment, when the baby was passed across to a young woman, also called Rose, and her husband Percy Sharp, there was concentrated a dense network of forces and causes, some global, others so private they were never spoken of again. The precise nature of Rose Wort's emotional turmoil in 1942 can only be guessed at. What we do know is that a catastrophic world war, whose outcome was still uncertain, had altered and was dominating all lives. It had removed from Rose her husband, Ernest, the father of her two children, and transformed him into an infantryman fighting in the North Africa campaign. It had brought into Rose's life a twenty-five-year-old, straight-backed sergeant major, David McEwan, whose own life had been radically changed; he had been injured in the Dunkirk evacuation of 1940 and had spent six months in Alder Hey Hospital. He was a sergeant, an instructor, but no longer considered combat fit. Ultimately the war was to remove Ernest from Rose's life altogether – he was fatally injured in action at Nijmegen in 1944. She and David McEwan married in 1947, and I was born the following year, not long before Rose went back into hospital for a hysterectomy.

Clearly, the lovers believed they had to conceal forever the living proof of their affair. Rose may have been hard up, and at times she and the two children were 'on the parish' – the pre-welfare state equivalent of social security benefit. She often spoke of how Ernest would disappear for long periods without explanation, leaving her without support. It's possible that in her affair with my father there was an element of tit for tat or entitlement. Certainly, her remarks to me many years later suggested that this was so.

For all that, she was a respectable young woman, and the closely knit village of Ash, just two miles from Aldershot, would have been outraged to see her bear another man's child when her husband was away at war. Rose would have faced the severest form of ostracism. Her love affair would have been seen as a deeply unpatriotic act. She would have dreaded Ernest's return and the inevitable terrible confrontation. Her child would have been stigmatised – 'born out of wedlock', 'illegitimate', 'bastard' – in a mere two generations these terms have lost their significance, and it is hard now for younger people to imagine their brutal, accusatory power. Total secrecy and complicated arrangements would have been necessary in order to keep knowledge of the pregnancy and the baby's existence from neighbours and family, and more importantly, from the children, Jim and Margy, then aged seven and five. For that reason they were sent away – Jim to spend the rest of his childhood with Ernest's mother, and Margy eventually to a harsh institution for servicemen's daughters where she almost died from an untreated illness. One way or another, all of us, all of Rose's four children, were sent away, and much of this had to do with my father.

He was a professional soldier, Glasgow born, a handsome,

muscular man with neat, Brylcreemed hair and a sergeant major's trim toothbrush moustache. As an unemployed seventeen-year-old, he had lied about his age to join the Highland Light Infantry in the early thirties. Now he was in the newly formed REME, the Royal Electrical and Mechanical Engineers. Off-duty he was convivial and liked to tell a good story and sing in the sergeants' mess. Domineering by nature, with a military taste for order and efficiency, he was feared by the men he trained. By his own account to me many years later, he found intimacy difficult, and was sexually innocent when he met our mother, and I have no reason not to believe him. To have a child by a woman whose husband was on active service overseas could have meant the ruin of Sergeant McEwan's army career — one more reason to do something quickly. That Ernest, the betrayed, died fighting for his country and the liberation of Europe while my father remained in barracks must have compounded the guilt and secrecy of later years.

Perhaps he was the one who forced the solution. Certainly, Rose would not have had the strength of character to stand in his way, and a woman of her class and generation would have had to go against the grain to pit her wil¹ against a man's. Or perhaps they were in it deeply together. Or again, just possibly, it may have been my mother, as the more vulnerable in the situation, who demanded drastic action. Whatever it was, the actual plan they settled on has much of my father about it. The advertisement in a local paper that offered a baby to any takers was ruthlessly terse. 'Complete surrender' carries a military echo – he may have hesitated to write 'unconditional'. The birth certificate that accompanied my brother to Reading Railway Station named Ernest Wort as the father. Was it a lingering paternal love, or vanity, or a little of both that prompted a father to give his baby the parting present of his own Christian name, as well as that of his own favourite brother, Stewart?

In the years since 2002 when I learned of my brother's existence, Margy, Jim (also known as Roy) and I have had time to reflect on the consequences this tightly held secret had for our family. Certainly, the pleasure and excitement of discovering a brother has to some extent been offset by a forced and continuing reappraisal of the past. In my own case, small instances keep offering themselves up for re-calibration: when I was nine my mother told me that I was never to mention in company that Margy and Jim had a different father from mine; when I interviewed my father on tape in 1989 and asked him to describe his first meeting with my mother, he became unaccountably angry – and so ended a half-hearted attempt to put together a family history; when, in 1987, I met Jim for a drink – a rare event in our fractured family – my parents were strangely nervous, my father especially plying me with questions the next day as though, it now seems, he thought Jim might have known too much; in the late nineties my mother told my cleaning lady that she, Rose, had once 'lost a baby'. Hearing this at second hand, I thought the reference was to a miscarriage and, carelessly, never followed it up. Now and then, small moments from the past like these demand re-interpretation.

The larger pattern seems a little clearer. It always baffled me why Jim was sent away to live with his granny, and I never received a satisfactory explanation until now. Only now do I fully understand that there was an unspoken, or rather, unconscious, rule in our family that the name of Ernest Wort was never to be uttered in my father's presence. David McEwan served abroad until his mid sixties, even though he had many opportunities to return to England. I wonder now if this was not a self-imposed exile. In 1959, at the age of eleven, I was sent from Tripoli, Libya to a state-run boarding school in England. Cut off from family, my parents' existence, especially in North Germany for the twenty years after 1961, seemed well ordered, and empty. They lived in married quarters on a variety of British Army camps and were profoundly bored and lonely. Occasionally they invited family out to join them and were extravagantly and exactingly hospitable. They watched German television at night, even though they did not understand a word. My mother occupied herself with the constant purchase and wrapping and dispatching of birthday and Christmas presents for even the remotest member of the family. She knitted for babies she would never meet. In retrospect, all that diligence, all that distance, seems immensely sad. So too does their failed attempt, years before in the mid-fifties, to adopt a child from a Dr Barnardo's home. I sometimes think their lives were haunted by the deed on Reading Station, and that the ghosts became more vivid as Rose and David grew older. I hope I am wrong.

My parents died with their secret. My father, among many things a companionable man who liked a drink, knew in his mid seventies that he was dying of emphysema; we passed many late nights together talking freely, but even the approach of the oblivion he was convinced of did not prompt him to speak. Rose lived on six years after he died and sometimes talked about her marriage in intimate, almost unbearable detail, but never of this. When her mind started to go, but while she had a decent portion of memory remaining, she spoke more of Ernest than of David, to whom she had been married for almost fifty years. But her growing confusion could not trick her into indiscretion. It is a poignant moment in my brother David's account, when she is at last re-united with the child she gave away, and she has no means left to her of understanding the occasion.

Against all the sadness was the simple fact of David's appearance. He found us by way of the Salvation Army. Lieutenant Colin Fairclough, who was coming to the end of a distinguished career and whose last case we were, handled his role as go-between with great sensitivity and wisdom. I shall always regard it as one of the strangest and most wondrous moments of my life, when I entered a pub on the edge of Oxford in February 2002 for a rendezvous with a brother I had never met. He was not difficult to spot; it was as though I was walking towards a mirror. Since there are no established conventions for such occasions (except, perhaps, at the end of a Shakespeare comedy), we were bound to fumble between a handshake and an embrace. There was further bathos when it took me more than a quarter of an hour to buy two glasses of wine at the bar. I kept glancing back over my shoulder at him, half expecting this apparition to fade. It is disconcerting, how quickly two lives can be summarised. We spoke for two or three hours. I was interested to discover what we had in common that could not be accounted for by experience alone: an aversion to tobacco, a tendency to develop basal cell carcinomas, and the interesting fact that we had stayed at the same hotel in Spain the preceding summer. A gene for hotel preference awaits expression.

David has not wandered far from Reading Station – south Oxfordshire is barely twenty miles away – but the story he tells is of a psychological distance travelled. What a relief it was to learn that first night that his adoptive parents loved him and looked after him well. He had all the information necessary to track down his biological family when he was twenty years old. I can understand why he hesitated then. His – that is, our – parents sent him a card on his first birthday, in 1943. Thereafter, apparently, silence. If they had not contacted him in nineteen years, so the young man reasoned, they would not be pleased to hear from him now. I like to think that in fact they would have been delighted and terribly relieved – a great burden of shame and silence would have been lifted. But of course, they could have lifted it for themselves. I am grateful to David for taking, as his sixtieth birthday approached, the difficult, risky decision to discover his origins at last. Not only have I acquired a brother, a sister-in-law, Julie and a niece, Marion, whose wedding to Gary (once a sergeant in the REME!) we were lucky enough to attend, I have also learned a great deal about the past. The cliché runs that there is no such thing as an ordinary family; I have had to live this long to find out just how strange ours really is.

Ian McEwan

PREFACE

There comes a time for every man when he sits down and takes stock of his life, looks at what he has accomplished so far, and what he hopes to do in the future. For most men it's probably between middle age and becoming a miserable old git. A time when, if your eyesight is still reasonably good, you may have your first glimpse of the grim reaper on the horizon, shuffling relentlessly towards you. For me, this time arrived in the late summer of 1998 when my daughter informed me I was going to be a granddad. The first thoughts that ran through my mind were that, when the time was right, I should tell my grandchild something about my life. Therefore, soon after Oliver's birth, I began to put pen to paper, recording events from my past. As I began this process, jotting down memories, making notes and slowly putting together a story of my life, little did I realise just what other remarkable chapters of that story were soon to unfold.

Dave Sharp

1

It seemed that in the late 1940s and early 50s everyone in our village kept a few chickens; not many, maybe a dozen birds at most. With rationing still in force most folks could keep themselves in eggs this way and when the birds stopped laying the owners would have an occasional roast chicken dinner. The chickens were fed primarily with left-over scraps from the house. The exception was at harvest time when the chickens' diet would be supplemented by corn. After the binder had been round to cut the corn and the sheaves were collected, there was generally an interval of a couple of weeks before the field was ploughed up. During this period people went out into the stubbled fields to go gleaning, which was picking up the ears of corn left behind by the binder. These ears of corn were then fed to the chickens.

One particular harvest time, when I was eight or nine years old, I was out gleaning in the fields with half a dozen friends, all about the same age as me. We had just started working a small area of the field, each of us making an individual pile of corn ears before putting them in our bags and moving on. Bent to our task, our keen young eyes searched out every detail of the soil. In our imaginations we were hunting for nuggets of gold and every glimmering sight of another stray piece of corn brought the joy of discovery and the pride of achievement to its finder. But gold prospectors are naturally competitive. As the sun rose higher over the field and each child's private harvest stacked up, as often happens with kids, an argument sprang up between a little blonde-haired girl and me concerning the ownership of a small heap of corn ears. 'Hey!' she said. 'Leave off, those are mine!' I looked at her. 'No, they're not,' I said, 'I've been piling mine up here for ages.' 'No, yours are over there, stupid.' 'No, these are mine,' I insisted. 'No, they're not!' 'Yes, they are!' 'Not!' And so it went on, our voices growing shriller, our bodies arched defensively, faces thrust pugnaciously at one another in passionate self-right-eousness. The whole quarrel was pointless, since the corn ears were to be shared out, but that didn't matter. What was at stake was who'd done the most work, and now that all the other children had gathered round neither of us was going to back down. It was a point of overweening childish honour that I was right and she was wrong. We stood irresolute, she a little older and taller, both of us with arms folded, lips angrily pursed and eyes trying to outstare the other. I wondered if we might come to blows and if not how this stand-off would end. We began to trade minor insults and as the store of unkind words and phrases became exhausted and we each struggled to outdo the last rude remark, my opponent came out with something that took me completely by surprise. 'Well,' she said loudly, 'at least I've got a proper mummy and daddy!' Her brother, who had been standing by her watching at this point turned and slapped her hard across the face, making her cry. 'They told us not to say anything about that in front of him,' he said. The girl held her cheek and now turned the full force of her anger on her brother. 'I'm telling mummy what you just did!' she said. She started crying now and turned to make her way across the field, heading for home. As she did so her brother shouted after her, 'Good, fuck off – and you can tell her why I did it.' Everyone in the cornfield fell silent and looked at me. I stared down and kicked at the stubble not knowing how to react to the little girl's remark or what to make of it. One by one the other children, who had stopped what they were doing to listen to the argument, now drifted off to carry on with their gleaning.

When I got back home with my bag of corn my mum had the dinner ready in the oven and Dad was washing his hands at the sink. 'Hello David,' said Mum. 'I'm just going to dish up. Have you been busy?' She looked at my bag of corn and smiled. 'Oh, he's been working his socks off!' said my dad, and ruffled my hair affectionately. 'He must be hungry as a hunter.' 'Sit down, love,' said Mum. 'How many potatoes would you like, David …?' It was just another teatime at 1,

3

Spring Terrace. When I'd cleaned my plate there'd be 'afters' of tinned fruit, and then Mum would wash up. Dad would put the radio on and in a few hours it would be time for bed. 'Night Mum – night Dad.' 'Goodnight David.' Everything was as it always was. What had that stupid girl in the field been on about? Of course I had a proper mummy and daddy. But that night, lying in bed and watching the candle cast its familiar shadows around my little room I felt sad, only I didn't know why.

2

A child's home is a child's world. However you live, all children live, so you imagine. If you're born in a castle you assume other boys and girls play in huge echoing banqueting halls, their laughter carrying down long, winding corridors. You don't even know they're huge or long or winding. It's just what's there. Castle children must think all houses contain libraries of books stretching high up to the ceiling with a ladder to reach them, and that turret rooms and a moat and a back yard the size of a soccer pitch are what every little boy has at home. It does not immediately cross the mind that others may live in far different surroundings. Not till a child reads or hears or sees for their self how other children live, do they realise that the world is a varied place.

Like most people, I did not grow up in a castle. Nor were there servants, rose gardens, drawing rooms or lawns so long you couldn't see where they ended — again, nothing uncommon about that. So what was my boyhood home like? You'll have already gathered there was no silver spoon in my mouth, though if you think this is going to be another story about a deprived childhood think again. Certainly there were a few hardships, but my family and I were by no means the only ones to experience them. And like I say, what you're used to doesn't seem arduous at the time. Everything's relative and even castle-dwellers have their problems — draughts, leaky roofs, upkeep costing an arm and a leg and the dilemma over which old master to part with when the west wing needs doing up. And for ordinary people, what were luxuries even fifty years ago are now seen as essential. Indoor toilets are today the most basic of facilities in British homes and families without central heating, a washing machine or a car are seen as living in the dark ages. Spare a thought too for any poor kid who doesn't have internet access or the latest pair of designer-label trainers.

Anyway, I'll stop beating about the bush now and tell you about my own life. Apart from birth to age one month, which I'll come to later, I spent my first two decades living at 1, Spring Terrace, Gravel Road, which is about six miles outside Reading in a village called Binfield Heath. There were four pubs, one on each corner as it were. These were the New Inn, the Coach and Horses, the George and Dragon and the Bottle and Glass, the latter being the only one that survives today. The area was what you might call a rural backwater, and looking back I would describe where I lived at that time as no more than a country slum. The house was on the end of a block of five, and had three bedrooms. Downstairs was gas lit, but for some peculiar reason there was no lighting upstairs. When it was time for bed I would be given a white candle in a red metal holder to illuminate my way aloft. Climbing the narrow wooden stairs, the candlelight casting eerie shadows up the walls, I would enter my bedroom, where the ill-fitting sash windows rattled and shook no matter how much newspaper my dad stuffed around the edge of the frame. The wind whistled through the gaps making the candle flicker and dance, and the shadows moved in continuous, shifting patterns over the ceiling and walls. Described like this I suppose it was what you might call creepy, but it never bothered me; it was simply normality.

Spring Terrace had a cold water tap and apart from that absolutely no other plumbing or sanitation at all. Even the washing-up water had to be taken outside and thrown on to the garden. How 'green' we were without realising it! Downstairs there were three rooms – a kitchen with a black grate, that, I seem to remember, was continually cleaned by Mum with some stuff called black lead. (I wonder if you can still buy black lead.) The focal point of the kitchen was the big iron range, where all the cooking was done. The range was heated by coal, which was delivered to our house by a Mr Povey who also ran the George and Dragon pub just down the road. We always stocked up on coal in the summer months as it was cheaper – come October the prices would always go up. My parents would usually buy a ton, which Mr Povey would drop off in sacks with corners turned like rabbits' ears. The coal would be emptied in the shed and the sacks counted to make sure the amount was correct. This was 'real' coal, not the perfectly formed oval nuggets of smokeless fuel common nowadays, but big rough-hewn chunks that chugged out real black smoke from the chimney.

Like many houses in the fifties there was no bathroom at Spring Terrace. We did possess a bath though, a long, galvanised one that hung from a nail outside the scullery window. Friday night was bath night, when the bath would be brought into the scullery while water was heated in the big copper that stood in the corner. When the bath had been filled I would take first turn and then be packed off to bed, after which my mum would bath and lastly my dad, all of us using the same water. The bathwater, like that used for the washing-up, would be tipped onto the garden. The water in the copper was heated solely by wood logs, which we got from the local woodman whose name was Den Belcher. Mr Belcher ran a family business. Or rather, he got his wife to hump the heavy sacks of logs off the lorry while he drove from house to house collecting the money from the customers. It wasn't only in fine weather that Mr Belcher gave his nearest and dearest this opportunity to keep fit and improve her complexion. Rain, hail or snow, she'd be out there trudging behind the lorry and heaving the logs on and off her shoulder. Obviously her husband was not what you'd call a paid-up member of the Women's Liberation movement.

Then again perhaps he was following the Soviet example, where women were already mending the roads and doing a lot of the heavy manual work. I never heard Mrs Belcher complain of her lot. She was probably too knackered.

'She looked lovely, didn't she?' said Aunt Grace. 'Oh yes, beautiful, really beautiful,' agreed my mum passing her sister-in-law a tea plate. They were talking about the newspaper pictures of Queen Elizabeth's coronation. 'Such a shame about her father though.' 'Yes, tragic for her, wasn't it – another cup of tea, Reg?' When I was young the front room was only used on special days like Christmas or when relatives came to visit. There weren't many visitors to the house, apart from my dad's brother Reg and his wife Grace who used to come up regularly from Henley-on-Thames for afternoon tea on a Sunday. My mum liked to cook, and was especially fond of baking cakes. Many are the times I remember us sitting down like this while Mum sliced up one of her Victoria sponges. The conversation was about the usual things – gardening, the weather. Sometimes they'd discuss current affairs, especially if there was some big national event, scandal or terrible crime in the papers. 'He looks so ordinary-looking, if you know what I mean,' was my mum's comment on John Christie, the Rillington Place murderer whose death sentence was announced a few weeks after the coronation. 'I'm not so sure, a nasty piece of work if you want my opinion,' demurred Aunt Grace. 'Well, you would say that now we all know what the man did,' said Uncle Reg leaping gallantly to Mum's defence. 'I mean if you know a chap's done in four women and hidden them under the floorboards he's bound to look shifty, stands to reason.' My mum gave a little cough at this and fiddled with some crumbs on her plate. 'Did they find out any more about the other three girls?' went on Uncle Reg. 'Apart from the fact they were all on the …' Now it was my dad's turn to cough and say to me briskly, 'Offer the plate round David, there's a good boy.' 'Yes, come on Grace, eat up,' joined in my mum, 'there's plenty more really.' Uncle Reg took the hint and asked, 'How are your tomato plants doing?' I don't think Mum and Dad were any more prudish than other people of their time; it was just accepted that there were certain things you didn't discuss in front of children, and in those days a ten-year-old was still considered very much a child. They always had the *Daily Mirror* delivered. I remember later on certain news items would prompt dark comments about 'the bomb' which it seemed was permanently pointed at us from Russia. We had one too, which we kept pointed at Russia. It was like a playground stand-off between them and us, the difference being that if a fight started it would kill everyone in the world. 'Last night I dreamt the bomb went off,' someone would say with a shiver of foreboding, or 'if the bomb goes off we won't need to worry about it' – 'it' being anything from the rising cost of living to the perennial problem of our draughty rattling windows. The *Daily Mirror* continued to provide our family with food for thought and I remember when I was in my early twenties rushing home to read it for the latest goings-on with Christine Keeler and Mandy-Rice Davis. That trial must have sold millions of newspapers and so provided a whole generation of spotty-faced kids with the only sex education they were likely to get.

I wasn't aware of my dad being strongly political in any way. During the war he'd had scarlet fever, which prevented him joining the forces. Instead he was on the fire watch over at Reading. With so many of the local husbands away on active service I feel sure there was a bit of resentment in the community directed at my parents. I often wonder if Dad was a pacifist, since he always hated violence of any kind, even reading about it in the newspapers or seeing it on the television. In all my life I never, ever heard him swear. Neither was he a big drinker at that time. Sometimes when we were out for a walk he'd stop off briefly at one of the village pubs for a packet of crisps and something to quench the thirst, and that was about it. Dad was a skilled tradesman, employed as a sheet-metal worker at the firm of Cope and Cope in Vastern Road, Reading. We did not have a car and he would cycle the five miles into work each morning, leaving the house at 7.30am in order to clock on by 8 o'clock. If you were three minutes late the time clock would automatically mark your card in red and a quarter of an hour's pay would be deducted from your wage packet at the end of the week. Clocking-off time was 5.30pm and Dad would cycle the five miles back again. In the summer months he often arrived home a little later since he would stop on the roadside and pick a bunch of wild flowers for my mum.

The house would often be bedecked with bunches of blue cornflowers contrasting with rich, red scabious.

The entertainment in our home was at first provided chiefly by the radio that stood on the living room sideboard. Although the radio contained a large battery it also had an accumulator, which was a large glass receptacle filled with a liquid, some kind of acid, I imagine. Each week the accumulator would need to be recharged and was taken down to Miller's paper shop, where Mr Miller would plug it into his mains supply. In the meantime we would use a second accumulator that had been left on charge the previous week. The programme I was especially fond of was 'Dick Barton, Special Agent'. Dick was an ex-wartime commando who now used his talents in the role of private eye-cum-special agent. Each week at 6.45pm, just after the news, Dick, together with his sidekicks Snowey White and Jock Anderson, would tangle with master villains, defeat their dastardly schemes and see that justice was done. I suppose the Dick Barton character was a blend of Sherlock Holmes and James Bond, though of course Bond was still a long way off then. Having said that, Dick was a gent to his fingertips, and unlike the Bond stories there was no sex, alcohol or swearing of any kind. There was violence, but it didn't go further than the occasional 'good, clean sock on the jaw'. Dick Barton's wholesomeness didn't stop the clergy and educationalists of the day from condemning it as immoral though. What would they make of today's popular entertainment one wonders, with porn and extreme violence as common as cookery programmes? At its peak the Dick Barton radio show played to an audience of 15 million. At the end of every story, avid listeners knew they could sleep safe in their beds, reassured that England was the country of fair play, and that crime never pays. I loved the programme, and looked forward excitedly to every episode. Everyone was familiar with the thrilling signature tune, which became synonymous with high-speed adventure, eleventh-hour rescue missions and tales of derring-do – in fact any kind of dramatic situation that drew listeners to the edge of their seats. The Dick Barton stories were adapted for TV and film, though the purists never really took to the visual versions. I suppose they already had their own imaginative picture of their hero, which no actor would ever quite resemble. Quite a bit later on my mum and dad brought a fourteen-inch black and white Ferguson television set, which took pride of place in the living room. At that time owning a TV was still relatively unusual. I don't know if it was by accident or design but our set was placed directly opposite the window. Passers-by could clearly see that we were keeping up with the Jones's, or maybe we were the Jones's, I don't know.

The Dick Barton of our own community was the local bobby Police Constable Insole, who covered both Binfield Heath and the neighbouring village of Shiplake. This was before policemen had been largely relegated to sitting in squad cars and PC Insole made his rounds sitting on a bicycle. Pedal power in those days however didn't mean a flashy aluminium mountain bike but the traditional 'sit-up-and-beg' model with the rod brakes and a steel frame like something Brunel would have spanned a gorge with. Picturing a rural constable on this solid conveyance might give the impression he was slow, and perhaps he was. But slow is not the same as ineffective. It certainly wasn't in PC Insole's case. Any lad who'd grown up in his manor knew that he was invariably in the right place at the right time – or for those up to no good, the wrong place at the wrong time. If you were doing something you shouldn't be – climbing the farmer's trees, a bit of scrumping or causing a nuisance in any way, you always had the feeling PC Insole was watching you and would soon be on the scene if you pushed your luck too far. Sometimes you didn't need to push your luck at all. His bicycle being well oiled it was invariably silent in its approach, and he would suddenly appear as if out of nowhere. Needless to say once Insole had collared you there was no form filling or mention of 'asbos'. On-the-spot punishment of a swift clip round the ear made the point and, yes, I know it's an old chestnut but it's a fact, if you went home and complained about what the copper had done, your dad would clip the other ear for you. Mind you we did manage to outwit Insole sometimes. When we were about fourteen going on fifteen, my mates and I used to cycle out to the White Hart in Shiplake to do a bit of under-age drinking. Since we knew Insole would look in on his rounds at some point in the evening, we always used to leave the back window of the pub open. That way we could sup up, keep our eyes peeled at the front, and scarper out of the back window if we saw the PC's bicycle approaching. The thing was, though, whenever this happened he must have known we'd been in the pub, because our own bikes would be leant up out the front.

Thomas Crapper's alleged invention of the flush toilet in 1898 was a major breakthrough in sanitation. However, half a century after its invention the WC had still not reached 1, Spring Terrace. Our toilet was a partitioned-off part of the wood shed, and consisted of a seat with a large bucket underneath. Bog-standard you might say. Once a week Dad would dig a hole in the garden and tip in the contents of the bucket. He would then fill the hole and put a stick into the top so he would know not to dig the same place the following week. The food chain was a short one in our garden and we always had a crop of fantastic potatoes. It was recycling at its most basic I suppose. Dad grew all sorts of other produce on his two allotments, which were each ten poles in size. Some readers will remember poles, if only from the back of old school exercise books where they were listed with all the other traditional units of measurement – rods, poles and perches, furlongs and chains. My dad would spend hours on his allotments, digging, planting and weeding. When I was about twelve he started collaring me to help out, and of all the jobs the one I detested most was thinning out the carrots and parsnips. However thinly sown they would always need to be thinned out later so they'd grow straight and long and not turn out all fingers and thumbs.

Thinning them was what you'd call labour-intensive – fiddly and backbreaking at the same time. The toil yielded results though, and the allotments used to keep us in fresh vegetables all year round. I can't ever remember us having to buy any vegetables from the shop. Again, like so many people we were 'green' before they invented the term, and the 'Good Life' had nothing on my Dad, although of course we did live in the country and not Surbiton like Tom and Barbara.

The outside toilet had no lighting so if you wanted to use it during the night you had to take a torch with you. One dark winter's evening when I was still a young boy I made my way out there and was just about to sit down when I heard a noise. Shining my torch I saw to my horror that a large rat had fallen into the bucket and was frantically swimming round and round trying to get out. I don't think I've ever moved faster, before or since. Even now I cringe when I think about it. If the rat hadn't been splashing I'd have plonked my backside straight down on the seat without looking. The rat would probably have used my little appendages to aid his escape, poor thing. It's enough to bring tears to your eyes – it would have mine. One early November night mum got a fright when she went out and discovered 'a man' sitting in the toilet. In fact it was a guy I'd made for Bonfire Night that I'd left in there.

The Spring Terrace house was very damp. I had pneumonia three times during my childhood, and bronchitis visited me every year without fail. The doctor always said I would grow out of it as I got older. I think he meant 'if' I got older. People may have nostalgic notions about that world of draughty windows, tin baths and candles to light you to bed, but I don't think nowadays I could endure the sort of conditions we lived in then. Not that I felt we were 'putting up' with anything really. There was just no thought of an alternative. It was the world I knew.

3

'It was *you*, wasn't it!'

The middle-aged face thrust itself at me accusingly, its cheeks puce with anger, the cavernous flared nostrils revealing a brush of thick black hairs. I was by now trembling, and felt my own cheeks burning with shame. I tried desperately to imagine what it was I had done wrong, but no thoughts would come, and my mouth, paralysed by fear, could find no answer. I stared silently up at the terrifying man, awaiting my punishment.

For the life of me I can't remember how I came to be involved in the first place. Maybe it was peer pressure. I mean, why, when I could have been out in the fresh air kicking a football around a field, had I joined a choir? Not that I'd had to attend an audition or anything like that to become a chorister at All Saints Church, Dunsden. It certainly wasn't *The X Factor*. On reflection I think they were glad to get anyone they could, and if there was a spare cassock that fitted, you were in. I must have been about eight or nine at the time. Every Thursday evening, together with three or four other little boys I would walk down the lane to All Saints and report for choir practice, and of course on Sundays we would don the heavy, long, black cassocks and white surplices for the morning service. I remember the church being quite well attended. There was no competition from DIY stores and supermarkets of course, nor were there outings to gastro pubs. Beefeaters and Harvesters were still decades away. Pubs did lunchtime trade but weren't open all day like now, and few served food. Going to the pub midday Sunday was mainly something men did (though not my dad then). At home their wives cooked the traditional roast, and before and during the meal would probably have the radio on for *Family Favourites*, *The Clitheroe Kid*, *The Navy Lark*, *Hancock's Half-Hour* or *Billy Cotton's Band Show*. Mostly, everything was closed on a Sunday and the nation was at rest (except for mum!) or worship.

In common with most churches, the choir sat up in the chancel area. On one side were the female choir stalls, with the demure little girls in the front tier and the ladies behind them. On the opposite side the 'angelic' boy choristers ummed and aahed and tried to keep in tune, while the men's choir wheezed along behind. After the service we would file quietly out in twos, make our way back to the vestry and disrobe before heading off cheerily to our homes for Sunday lunch. This Sunday however something very different had happened. No sooner had we reached the vestry than the choirmaster ordered all the boys outside. Even then I could see he looked a bit angry – 'a bit' is an understatement to say the least – he was steaming. While the vicar was shaking hands with his parishioners at the main door, we obediently gathered on the little grassy path alongside the vestry. Some of the boys looked a bit nervous, while others were smirking slyly at one another. The thought that someone might be in trouble – so long as it wasn't them – was a bit of excitement to liven up the usual Sunday routine. The choirmaster, his face still looking like it was going to explode, glared at us in the midday sunshine and bawled, 'Well, who did it?' None of us said a word. What was he talking about? Our combined silence made him even angrier; he was a big man who towered over us at the best of times, now, fired up, he looked enormous. His complexion had rapidly changed to the puce horror mask that now glowered within inches of my face, and beads of sweat had formed on his forehead. The choirmaster had looked in turn at each boy, his fierce eyes burning into theirs before finally resting his gaze on me. In all my young life I swear I had never seen anyone so angry. He repeated the mysterious, menacing accusation, the inflexion in his voice this time demanding that I admit my guilt: 'It was *you*, wasn't it?' His breath smelt awful, a mixture of horseshit and damp bus tickets, if you can imagine that. Maybe it was something he'd had for breakfast, but whatever it was it was turning my stomach; that and the fear. Again I tried to think whether I'd been mucking about at all in church that day and what he might have seen. But my mind was still a terrified blank and all I could do was look down nervously at my shoes. Finally he named my crime. 'It was you who farted in church, wasn't it?' The words were spat out like machine-gun fire. I knew it wasn't me, in fact I was bloody well certain of it, but that didn't matter. I could still be in trouble for it, and I knew that when an adult accused you of something so vehemently there was little point in arguing even if you had the courage, which I didn't. At that moment I was just so in awe of this huge man, his white surplice making his puce face look even pucer. It was like something out of a Boris Karloff film. He then said in the same rat-a-tat voice, 'I don't want to see you here ever again,' and with that he turned and stomped off back into the vestry. So that was that – thrown out of the choir for a fart I never did. Gone with the wind you could say. The moment we boys were on our own the blame game started, but not one of them would take responsibility for the phantom fart and no one ever did. For all anyone knew it could have been a member of the congregation. Maybe during the hymns one of them hit a bum note.

Many years later, when I was in my twenties, I was in the pub having a laugh and a pint or three with one of those former choir mates. We reminisced over the phantom fart and he told me that they had found out that the assistant choirmaster had been the guilty party. Apparently it transpired that he had a 'problem in that department'. He could have owned up. If I'd not been sacked from the choir who knows what musical heights I might have soared to, ending up like Aled Jones perhaps. Now there's a thought. Both my mum and dad are buried in the All Saints churchyard, and when I'm tending their graves I often think back and smile to myself as I pass that vestry door. Few people go through life without being wrongly accused of things far worse than an involuntary bodily function, but why the choirmaster had been so angry and why he had singled me out is a mystery.

Leaving the choir gave me more time for football and generally romping in the great outdoors, especially in the summer months. This was an era when it was still normal for children to wander miles from home and be out for hours, sometimes all day long, particularly if you lived in the country. This wasn't because our parents were irresponsible – it was just the way things were. We were given the same warnings as kids today with regard to strangers, and with far fewer people owning cars, any strangers coming into a rural community stuck out a mile. Like any place, town or country, there were also 'strangers' living amongst us; neighbours and other local residents we knew of, and who knew us, but that we didn't mix much with. In general terms, your particular tribe, if you like, can be defined by your occupation, the size of your house, whether it's a semi or a detached, or even something as simple as which end of the road you happen to reside in. And England being England, we tend to live and let live with our less familiar neighbours, so long as certain boundaries aren't crossed. And the story that follows shortly offers, shall we say, a concrete example of this.

As kids, my friends and I were aware of families in our local area who were well off. They were the ones who lived in the big houses with 'grounds', and who had chauffeurs and gardeners and nannies that you only saw now and again, entering or leaving through big iron gates. Peering at these opulent dwellings from the roadside as we sauntered idly by, my young friends and I didn't feel hard-done-by. Our 'grounds' were far larger, extending as far as we could wander in a day, with every tree along the lane ours for the climbing. Our ceiling was infinitely higher than any house too, being the sky over our heads. By and large children aren't so interested in things the grown-up world holds in esteem. Who, as a child, would want to be cooped up behind a high wall, with manicured lawns, and servants keeping their beady eyes on you all the time? There was however one occasion when certain benefits enjoyed by the wealthy proved too tempting for us to resist. When, each July, we broke up from school, the six weeks of liberty that stretched out ahead of us seemed like one glorious, unending treat. Great for us kids, yes, but inevitably we got bored sometimes. This was before the advent of package holidays, with cheap flights taking families to the Costa Brava or the Costa del Sol for a fortnight of Watneys' Red Barrel, Sangria and 'Kidz Clubs' every summer. With no such change of scene to break up the routine, time could hang heavily, and when kids have no work or diversion for their idle hands and high spirits, the devil will always help out. It was a gloriously hot August day, the temperature probably well into the eighties, when two mates and myself were strolling past a big house whose perimeter wall bordered the lane. It was just after midday, and with the sun high in the sky, and having already walked several miles, we were by now absolutely baking. With the sweat pouring off us, we would have loved nothing more at that point than to strip to our underpants and jump into a pond or stream to cool off. There was no natural feature of this kind nearby however. Finding a little strip of soft grass between the side of the lane and the wall of the big house, we flopped down to rest. 'What I wouldn't give for a swim right now!' said one of my mates with a deep sigh. 'I'm boiling,' said my other friend. 'Here,' I said. 'You know where we are, don't you?' and jerked my thumb behind us, towards the wall surrounding the house. 'Oh yeah ...' said the other two. 'And you know what's in there, don't you?' I said. In the grounds of the house, just a couple of hundred yards or so from where we were sat, was a large, open-air and very private, swimming pool. We had glimpsed it one time when mischievously scaling the wall. I could tell from my mates' faces they remembered the pool too, and that we were all now thinking the same thing. On such a scorching day, to take a dip in the cool water of that pool would be sheer ecstasy. We didn't need to think about it for very long. With furtive glances up and down the lane, we ran at the wall, helping each other to find foot- and handholds, and scrambled up eagerly. Reaching the top we stopped. Three chins were pressed onto the brickwork, three pairs of eyes peered cautiously over. In the distance the big house stood silent and imposing, its rows of windows staring back, watching, as if daring us to come closer. In the foreground, guarded by statues of ancient gods set at regular intervals in the flagstones, motionless as a millpond and glistening in the sunlight like a long, flat rectangular mirror, was the pool. There was no one about by the house or in the grounds, the only sign of life a solitary wheelbarrow and a spade, left dug into a mound of earth next to the flowerbeds. The gardener was presumably on his lunch break. 'Come on,' we all three said together under our breath. In another ten seconds we were over the wall and running across the lawn. At the edge of the pool we flung off our shoes, trousers, shirts and socks, 'shushing' each other in between nervous, suppressed laughter, and lowered ourselves carefully into the water. After the brief gasp-inducing shock of entering the cold water on such a hot day, the experience proved as good as we had anticipated, and it felt delicious to be immersed, especially after the exertion of climbing the wall and the mad dash over the lawn. Surrendering to the water's silky embrace, we all three glided out quietly with gentle strokes to the centre of the pool. There is an old saying, often used of apprentices, that one boy is a boy, two boys half a boy and three boys no boys at all. All it means is that whenever and wherever boys get together in a pair or a group, they tend to be self-forgetful and more often than not start to lark about. My friends and I were no exception that day. Exhilarated by the adventure and the refreshing effect of the water, we soon began to get noisy. A playful splash from one of my mates led to a vigorous retaliation from the other, and it was immediately all onto all, with water sloshing over the edge of the pool onto the paved pathway. Before long we were climbing out and repeatedly dive-bombing one another, causing huge tidal waves, and equally huge shouts and cries of excitable laughter. We had completely forgotten where we were, and more importantly, that it was somewhere we most definitely weren't supposed to be. We had crossed a boundary, in more ways than one. As our high-spirited games rose to a crescendo, another sound suddenly cut through the cacophony rising around the pool. It was a woman's voice, and it was shrill with anger. 'Hey, you filthy little boys! What on earth do you think you're doing?' We looked up to see, stood on the flagstones at the edge of the pool, as rigid and stony-faced as the ancient mythical statues that flanked her on either side, a prim, elderly lady glowering down at us. We had been so lost in our games we had not even seen her approach. For an instant we froze in shock, then leapt out of the pool, snatched up our clothes and with our baggy, dripping underpants clinging to us, made hell for leather for the wall. We ran some way down the road before halting to catch our breath, put our clothes back on, and, now we were safe, laugh in triumph. We had stolen a march on the rich people in the big house, swum in

27

their pool, and gotten away with it. Our injuries were no more than the odd scratch and bruise from hurling ourselves over the wall. No doubt the lady's only intention had been to shame us into running away, and in this she had succeeded. I suppose we were lucky there had been no dogs on the loose. What we heard later, though, suggested that, if the staff at the house had caught up with us, we might have got more than a ticking off. Being a village, news of the incident went round like wildfire, especially since the gardener who worked at the house lived locally. It was he who reported that, after we had scarpered, the owners had immediately ordered the huge pool to be completely emptied, thoroughly cleaned and refilled again. Presumably, as when burglars break in, they had felt a sense of intrusion at finding three boys, albeit in a spirit of innocent fun, taking liberties on their property. They must have wanted to feel that all trace of us had been cleaned away.

Most of my term-time days were of course taken up by school. I remember my class at Rotherfield had fifty-eight kids on the register. Many of the male teachers had a few years previously been demobbed from the forces at the end of the war. After a crash course at teacher training college they were thrown in at the deep end to deal with classes far too large for them to handle. The only way they could control a class of that size was by violence and the threat of violence. It is my opinion that many of the teachers were still traumatised from what they had witnessed during the war. Today they would have received counselling to help them get over their ordeals but such things were unheard of then. These ex-forces teachers also brought the mindset of the military with them, and the aggressive discipline they'd previously been on the receiving end of. Our English teacher in particular had a unique way of encouraging us to become perfect at spelling. For every spelling mistake we would receive, boys and girls, one whack across the arse with a plimsoll. (The tabloids would have a field day if that happened today.) Even in those far-off days, six strokes was the maximum that could legally be administered, so sometimes if you got, say, nine spellings wrong you would receive six whacks one day and the remaining three the next. I was a long way from being the best at spelling in the class and as we had English three, maybe four times a week, I was generally in line for a beating. When I woke up in the morning the dread of the slipper filled my mind, as it did really hurt and afterwards generally made you cry. Going to school could be traumatising to say the least. However, one day the opportunity arose for me to reduce my spelling misdemeanours and consequently sit without discomfort. Whether or not it was a habit acquired while he was fighting for king and country I don't know (and of course during the war smoking had been recommended to 'calm your nerves'), but our teacher was completely hooked on nicotine. He just could not manage without his fags, or to be more precise, his Player's Weights. Anyway this particular day, as the condensation covered the windows of the classroom and the rain beat down outside, our teacher

announced, 'I need someone to run an errand for me.'
Everyone in the class knew what he needed, another
nicotine fix. No one said a word. The rain was becoming
even more torrential, bucketing it down and lashing against
the windows. Who'd want to go out in that lot? I looked at
the blackboard and saw that there were fifteen words to
learn – I would be lucky to get half a dozen of them right.
My hand shot up. 'I'll go sir.' I figured it would be better to
get soaking wet than to get that slipper again. 'Have you got
a coat, Sharp?' 'Yes sir.' I didn't, but I didn't care – anything
to get out of that classroom. 'Good. Here, go to The Dog
and get me twenty Player's Weights and don't lose the
change.' 'Yes sir.' From that day forth I always got his fags.
The pub was about a quarter of a mile away. By the time I'd
sauntered down the road and back the lesson was over. On
future errands, if it wasn't I'd hide in the toilets until the bell
sounded. Of course the down side of it was that to this day
my spelling remains crap.

We did have a very nice Literature teacher who controlled
us not with the stick but with the carrot of stimulating
lessons. She spent a long time with us on the story of Don
Quixote, and the way she presented it really brought the
adventures of this funny little knight to life. I can still
remember the name of his horse, Rosinante, though I can't
actually remember what this teacher was called. Maybe that's
a credit to her that her lessons stayed in my mind long after
I forgot her name. Anyway what I do remember is that all
the class was disappointed when she left. The day her

replacement took over began as a sad one for us. 'Right class, now for this first lesson I want to introduce you to the book we will be studying this term. It is in some ways a difficult read with many layers, but there is a lot we can learn from it, so I hope you all like a challenge and are prepared to work hard.' Inwardly we all groaned. Sure we liked a challenge, but we liked resting on our laurels more. *Don Quixote* had been such fun and we'd got to know it backwards with our old teacher; now we were going to be asked to work! 'Turn to a new page and copy this down into your exercise books,' said our new teacher, and turned towards the blackboard. As she began to chalk up the first word a little murmur ran round the classroom. By the time the second word was finished we were smiling. 'There,' she said. '*Don Quixote*. Now, let me tell you a little about the story ...' No one said a word and we were soon a model Literature class, the quickest of learners and brimming with facts. 'What is the name of Don Quixote's companion?' 'Sancho Panza, Miss.' 'Where is the novel set?' 'In medieval Spain, Miss.' 'What is one of the main themes of the book?' 'Chivalry, Miss.' 'Give me an example of Don Quixote's foolishness.' 'When he tilts at the windmills, Miss.' ... 'written around 1600, Miss ... Miguel Cervantes, Miss ... three bags full, Miss ...' It was like we were all on *Mastermind* and sailing through our specialist subject with no passes. Then one morning a boy pipes up, 'Miss, we did *Don Quixote* last term.' He was popular. From then on our teacher had the audacity to teach us things we didn't know.

4

Certain events in life stay with you. No matter how long ago they occurred you are always able to bring them back. For me, one such occasion was the early summer of 1957 when I was coming up to fifteen.

'David – come on, or you'll be late.'

'Hmm, all right Dad,' I murmured. I was already awake. The dawn chorus in the hedgerow had made sure of it. The day was starting out just like any other. Every morning my dad would call me at this time, about 6.15am. By the time I got downstairs the tea was made and on the kitchen table, the milk in the cups. My mum was still in bed. Although my dad was not an educated man he always drummed into me the value of the 'work ethic' – early to bed, early to rise, the work won't do itself, hard work never hurt anyone … The attitude has stayed with me all my life, and even now I feel guilty if I don't go to work. There seems nothing worse than watching the rain coming down when I've got a wall to build or a patio to lay. Anyway that morning there I am having a quick cup of tea and then off down the road on my bike. The air is sweet, the fields moist with dew. By 6.40am I arrive at the village shop. 'Ding–ding' goes the shop bell as I enter. 'Morning David,' says Mrs Miller, knelt down over several stacks of newspapers, and marking them up with the names and addresses of customers. Mr and Mrs Miller have kept the shop for years. I pick up the large satchel and gather up my allocated papers. I had in fact two paper rounds to do each morning, the first taking me to the centre of our village, after which it was back to the shop to pick up a second lot of papers for delivery in the adjoining village of Dunsden. Knowing the route by heart I had everything done and dusted and was soon pedalling back home. It was now 8 o'clock and my mum was up as usual and had a breakfast of cereal, toast and a fresh pot of tea ready for me on the table. After breakfast I kissed my mum goodbye and went to meet up with my mates for the half-mile walk back into the village, passing the bakers and the blacksmith to the stop for the coach, which would take us to Rotherfield Grays Secondary School.

The school day passed normally. Once back home my routine was the same whatever the time of year – in for tea and then out with the football. I don't think the pleasures of homework had reached Rotherfield Secondary School, at least I don't recall ever being set any. Maybe some kids did and the teachers had just given up on me. I'd usually stay outside kicking about till dusk and that night was no exception. The sun had already dropped behind the trees as I heard my dad calling me from the house. 'David – could you come on indoors now?' 'Coming ...' I answered, still toeing the ball in the fading light. My dad called again, which wasn't strange in itself, but this time something was different for he added, 'We've got something to tell you.' Trapping the football I stood there in the empty field for a moment trying to think if I'd been doing anything I shouldn't recently. I then picked up my ball and ran indoors. As soon as I entered the kitchen I knew this was no longer a normal day; in fact it was quite unlike any other day in our home. The atmosphere in the room was electric. My mother was standing behind one of the upright chairs. The first thing I noticed was her hands, which were gripped tightly on the back of the chair. I looked at her face and saw that there were big tears rolling down her face. What was going on? 'Don't tell him,' said my mum in an anguished sob, 'there's no need.' My dad who was standing on the opposite side of the room, the solid table separating them said quietly, 'I've got to, he's got a right to know.' I felt my heart start to race. Know what, what were they on about? I looked from one to the other. My dad stared at the floor, my mum clenching a handkerchief, her face puckered with pain. I felt the room sway around me. Finally my dad spoke. 'Son, we both love you more than we can say – but, well, the thing is this: we are not your real parents.' The last words were blurted out, as if he was ridding himself of some burden. My mum immediately rushed across the room and threw her arms tightly around my neck. 'Please, don't turn against us David, please don't,' she pleaded. 'I'm sorry, we always meant to tell you but ... but we just, put it off ...' She was now sobbing violently, her ribcage straining as emotion wracked her whole body. I felt her hot tears falling on my face. On the wall was an oblong mirror with the corners bevelled off. It was a familiar object in our kitchen that had been there as long as I could remember, but now I saw something completely different reflected in it, the back of my mum's head burying against me. As she nuzzled tighter I caught a glimpse of my own face. It was like a blank mask, my own and not my own. 'Of course I won't,' was all I could say. My dad went to the cupboard and opened the left-hand drawer. He took out a brown envelope, withdrew a piece of paper and handed it to me. 'It says your name – was – Stewart, Stewart David Wort,' he mumbled awkwardly. My mother who was now sitting hunched at the table gave an agonised gasp, her shoulders heaving as a fresh bout of tears burst forth. I peered down at the faded paper. 'It's your birth certificate,' said my dad. I read the name he had said, 'Wort,' and thought how strange it sounded. 'Surrey South-Western District' was also written on the form. My dad moved around to the other side of the table and put his arms around my mum as she continued to cry. I said nothing. I could say nothing. I put the piece of paper down on the table, then turned and made my way up to my little bedroom. Although the window was open the room seemed airless. I could hear the breeze rustling the leaves on the apple tree outside. Somewhere in the far distance a dog was barking. Downstairs I could still hear my mum sobbing. It was now dark. I lay on my back on my bed and stared into the blackness. My mum, she was the rock in my life, always there for me. And now I'd repaid her love by making her cry. It was all my fault. I wished more than anything I hadn't made her cry. I closed my eyes and felt tears gathering, which soon overflowed and ran down my face. There was no stopping them. I felt I had somehow let both my mum and dad down. Such was the trauma and sadness of that night that the subject became taboo, and no one spoke of it again.

5

'Tinker, tailor, soldier, sailor, rich man, poor man, beggar man, thief.' My dad's finger slowed ominously as it reached the last prune stone on the side of my plate. This was the worst fate it seemed, to be a thief, and there was the sense that if you didn't look sharp, you'd automatically slip to the bottom of the heap. Did that mean the beggar man was second worst and tinker the most desirable occupation? 'What's a tinker?' I asked. 'Like a gipsy,' said my mum, clattering plates in the sink. Mum always seemed to be washing up. 'A tinker's someone who sells things,' my dad said. What never seemed clear with the prune game was whether you chose your stone or it chose you.

'Reading town centre please,' I said to the bus conductor, who took my sixpence and three pennies and turned the handle of his ticket machine. Being almost fifteen and soon due to leave school I was off to arrange my future. The prune stones of life were about to be examined and it was time to see which would be mine. Nowadays there are careers officers providing guidance to children about the different vocational choices on leaving school. In the fifties we didn't have careers officers, though we did have what was called a 'youth employment officer', probably the same meat, just different gravy. That year of 1957, Harold Macmillan had just been made prime minister. 'Supermac', as they called him, was replacing Anthony Eden who'd got all the stick for sending the gunboats into Suez the year before. The world was changing and Britain didn't rule the waves so easily any more, or waive the rules. But at home things were said to be getting better for the average bloke and his family. Three years earlier rationing had ended and some people actually burnt their ration books they were that pleased. Macmillan got on his soapbox and told the British people how well off they were. Tommy Trinder's catchphrase used to be, 'You lucky people!' Macmillan had come out with a similar one. Reminding everyone about the plentiful jobs, the welfare state and all the wonderful opportunities there now were for British people, he told us, 'You've never had it so good.' At fifteen I hadn't had it at all, and neither had I been out to work yet. But there was a big wide world beckoning from beyond the school gates and I was intrigued to find out what it had in store for me.

My school had arranged the appointment for me to meet one of these youth employment officers who covered my area. He was based in Reading so it meant taking a day off classes to go along and see him, which was no great shame. Naturally it was a bit of an adventure to catch the number 8 bus from Binfield Heath while lesser mortals were still in lessons. The place I'd been asked to report to was over by Reading Railway Station, in Gun Street close to where, at the time of writing this, the Café Mal now sits. That year, 1957, happened to be the one that rock and roll first rolled into Britain. A twenty-year-old ex-merchant seaman called Tommy Hicks changed his name to Tommy Steel and had a hit with 'Singing the Blues', while Bill Haley and his Comets had come over from the States in February and rocked us around the clock. With his comb-over hairstyle and middle-aged sort of look, Haley was hardly the devil incarnate that respectable people thought rock and roll represented. You wonder how he'd have gone down in the music pubs nowadays on a Friday night. Anyway, I got myself along to this youth employment officer's place, and entering the office the first thing I noticed sitting on the bloke's desk was the form I had filled in at school. Well, I say filled in. As I hadn't a clue what kind of job I wanted most of the form was still blank. When I'd first been given it I remember quite clearly asking my dad what I should put down as my 'desired occupation' or however they'd phrased it. His advice to me was simple: 'Do whatever makes you happy,' he said. Now that's very good and kind advice, but how do you follow it?

The youth employment officer for the Reading area was

a thin, balding, middle-aged man with yellow teeth and an ill-fitting grey suit. He asked me to sit, and then picked up my form. Obviously not needing long to read it he put it back down and peered at me through his little round National Health glasses, the kind a lot of teachers and government clerks seemed to wear in those days. He then turned to a wooden card-index box on his desk and began flipping through it. Reading one of the cards he said, 'Do you want to work in an office?' My eyes scanned quickly around the dreary room, taking in the filing cabinets, the stained ink blotter, the desk calendar, the heavy clock, and most of all, the four walls. I'd be climbing them after a few days. Talk about claustrophobia. If this was office work then no thanks. 'No,' I said. 'How about shop work?' he said looking at another card. At this I pictured myself slicing up bacon behind a counter or measuring inside legs in some stuffy gents' outfitters – definitely not my scene either way. 'No, not shop work,' I said. The youth employment officer continued to flick through his index box. Suddenly he stopped. Pulling out a card he studied it for an age then said, 'I noticed on your form that you would prefer to work outside.' Yes, I remembered putting that down; it was one thing I was fairly sure of. 'Then how about ...' he said, smiling and taking the card from the box with a little flourish, like some third-rate conjuror performing a trick, '... a job in the oil industry?' Hmm, that definitely sounded more interesting. 'But I must warn you,' he went on, 'this position does involve a great deal of travelling.' The oil industry, travel! At hearing these words my mind summoned up pictures of far-away places I had seen in magazines – blue skies, sun, sandy beaches, jetting off here there and everywhere. Perhaps they wanted someone to deal with 'gushers' in the Texas oil fields, or maybe it was an executive post with a big American motor, a secretary and a ten-gallon hat. Either way it sounded exciting, amazing. 'Yes, I'll take it.' I thought I'd better say yes straight away in case whichever bugger had the next appointment that day took it instead. Jobs in the oil industry don't come to Reading youth employment office that often. 'When can I start?' I said. 'Well, you could start tomorrow if you like.' Tomorrow, bloody hell, I thought. Well I wanted the job, no doubt about that, but I'd have to sort a few things out first. I might have been a naive fifteen-year-old kid but I knew you needed a passport to travel to other countries, and a passport was something I didn't have. I imagined they'd understand that though, and give me time to get it all organised. The youth employment officer for Reading was tapping the card on his desk impatiently. 'Well,' he said, 'yes or no?' 'Yes,' I said. 'But I can't start tomorrow, I've got to get a passport.' He looked at me. 'Passport?' he said. 'Yeah, I haven't got one.' I was already feeling crestfallen. By the way he was looking at me I could tell they had to have someone who could start right away. If I'd applied for a passport beforehand I could have had the job, but how was I to have known? 'No, no,' the officer was going on. 'You won't need a passport, the job's based right here in Reading.' He then cleared his throat and read aloud from the index card, 'To assist with deliveries of domestic heating fuel in and around the Tilehurst (Reading suburbs) area. Some lifting involved – must be fit and hardworking. Suit school leaver, overalls supplied ...' What he was offering me was a job as a lorry driver's mate delivering paraffin, the wanker. I made it clear I didn't want the job, telling him in my best industrial language where he could stick his index card, and left. When I got outside the thought crossed my mind that he probably pulled that trick several times a day on any gullible kid who would listen. Winding them up like that I suppose helped him to get through his otherwise boring day of watching the clock.

Perhaps it was my imagination but everyone seemed to have a job in those days. In the 1950s if you didn't put in a fair day's work for a fair day's pay you were regarded as work-shy, a dosser, a layabout, a loafer, sponger, leech or downright lazy good-for-nothing ****. 'Idle bastard' was also not unheard of. The work ethic, for good or bad, made decent people feel ashamed if they weren't in gainful employment of some kind. Being on National Assistance was definitely a stigma, even for people who genuinely couldn't work through no fault of their own, and it was a matter of pride that you paid your way. After I'd left school, having turned down that golden opportunity to hump cans of paraffin round the streets, it soon got to the stage where all of my mates had got jobs and I was in danger of being the idle so-and-so. So it was with a hint of desperation that I found myself one morning outside the firm of Cope and Cope in Vastern Road, Reading, the factory where my dad was employed as a sheet-metal worker. I hadn't told him I was coming. I hadn't got an appointment either. I just walked into the front office and asked for a job. After being interviewed for the best part of five minutes I was told I could start as an electrical engineering apprentice but first I'd be on a three months' trial. My dad was pleased I had a job at last; after all, by this time it was a month since I'd left school. He was even more pleased that I would be working at the same place as he was.

The part of the factory I was to work in was above the main premises and had to be reached by climbing a steep flight of stairs. Cope and Cope were manufacturers of various types of equipment for the poultry industry – incubators, cages for battery hens, that sort of thing. The section I'd been assigned to work was where the chicken 'de-beakers' and stunners were made. A de-beaker is like a large pair of pliers with a blade, inside which there is also a heating element. The de-beaker is used to cut off the chicken's beaks so they don't pull each other's feathers out while stuck in the endless rows of cages laying eggs. (A battery farm I imagine is a bit like one of these telephone call centres nowadays, except the chickens, having more brains, aren't pestering people in their homes and trying to flog them mortgages or mobile phones.) The 'stunners', sadly, were not bathing beauties or glamour models (there were none of those working at Cope and Cope, but I'll come to that later). A chicken stunner consisted of a transformer which was plugged into the mains and had another cable connected to a razor-sharp knife with an insulated handle. When the chickens were sent to the slaughterhouse they were hung upside down, still alive, from a conveyor belt. The belt was moving continuously, and as each bird reached the stunner the operator would press a button that activated the knife-blade and at the same time sent a current down the cable. This would cut the chicken's throat and give it an electric shock at the same time. Belt and braces I suppose. I imagine this is how euthanasia will be carried out on the retired population in fifty years' time when there aren't any pensions any more.

Working in my section was the boss of the factory, a man called Norman Fry. It was said that Norman had once been a singer with the Billy Cotton Band, and he could often be heard exercising his vocal chords on the shop floor. He didn't have what you'd call an extensive repertoire though. In fact he only seemed to know one song, the theme from *Casablanca*, 'As Time Goes By'. This lack of musical variety was probably why he was no longer touring the globe in the glamorous world of show business but manufacturing chicken-slaughtering equipment in Reading. Every now and again, day in day out, you could hear Norman's dulcet tones in between the thud of machinery and crash of metal, '… it's still the same old story, a fight for love and glory …' It was still the same old song too. No one ever said 'Play it again Norman.' Then there was the foreman, the one who

was directly responsible for keeping me busy. If I looked idle
at any time, he'd find something for me to do, whether it
needed doing or not. Is it Murphy's Law that says 'work
expands to fill the time available for its completion'?
Whoever said it first, the foreman at Cope and Cope
certainly believed in it, but he wasn't a bad old stick for all
that, and so long as I looked busy he left me alone.

Apart from Norman and the foreman there were no other
men in my part of the factory. It was the other workers who
were to give me the real grief – the women. Up until I
walked through those factory doors as a fifteen-year-old I
had always called women 'Mrs', even women in their mid
twenties and not married I'd call 'Mrs'. That's the way it was,
the way I'd been brought up I suppose. I remember one time
out on my paper round I'd had to collect the week's money
from a customer. I'd knocked on the door and when it
opened there was this lady stood there. I can only describe
her as large, and she was dressed in nothing but a bath towel.
In fact she was very large – think Hattie Jacques. She smiled
at me. 'Oh, thanks duck,' she said, taking the paper while
clasping the towel together behind her in her other hand. 'I
was asked to pick up the ...' I began. Remembering she said,
'Ooh, sorry yes, I've got to pay my debts, haven't I! I won't
keep you a minute love.' She then turned back into the hall
and as she did so it became clear that the towel did not match
her dimensions. Though still clutching everything together
to conceal her front, the back of the material yawned open
to the four winds and the gaze of anyone who might be

passing. Fortunately or unfortunately, at that hour of the morning there was only me. The gap in the towel was filled by two huge haunches, fleshy and animated. As she rummaged through a drawer for change the two moving hams wobbled and undulated. When I got home that morning I ate less breakfast than usual. This had so far been my only encounter with the unclothed female form. I was, frankly, as naive, green as grass and wet behind the ears, as they come. Apart from the lady in the towel, who may have been quite unaware of her exposure and had certainly made no suggestive remarks, the women at Cope and Cope were a bit different to the ones I'd come across before. From the moment they arrived at work till the time they clocked off at night there was only one topic of conversation that passed their lips – sex. At my tender age I just could not believe the things they kept coming out with, and being as I was the only young lad amongst them, I used to get bloody embarrassed I don't mind telling you. Because my discomfort was so obvious they would take great delight in seeing me squirm, and though they would talk about me as if I wasn't there, they knew full well my teenage ears were burning at every other word. The most popular topic of conversation when they discussed me in this way was my own sex life, or the lack of it. Nowadays when you hear people talking about the 1950s it's always about how repressed everyone was and how no one mentioned sex. This lot mentioned little else. It was also an open secret around the factory that two of these 'ladies', Pat and Jill, had an additional source of income from moonlighting as prostitutes at the nearby Greenham Common US Air Force Base. Pat was plain speaking, 'brassy' and a suicide blonde (dyed by her own hand) and Jill her sidekick was mousier but just as mouthy. Together they were formidable, a pair of slimline Mae Wests except there wasn't a gun in my pocket and I was never pleased to see them. As soon as they arrived on the shop floor in the morning, bleary-eyed from their nocturnal activities, I knew it wouldn't be long before they would sidle over to my workbench to embarrass me with the most intimate details of their latest escapades with clients. 'The one I had last night told me he was from Nevada – I said never mind Nevada dear, what's getting 'arder? One Yank and they were down! D'you get it Davey? Oh look at his face, Jill – ha-ha-ha, oh crikey …!' Ha-ha bloody ha.

After three months the crunch came. It was a Friday, mid summer, and very hot. The sun pitched down onto the factory's asbestos roof that absorbed and magnified the heat, raising the temperature even higher. By noon the factory was like an oven, airless, oppressive, suffocating, and I was burning up mentally as well as physically. When lunchtime arrived I found myself alone in the factory, Norman and the foreman having knocked off for an hour and the female gang also having a break together somewhere. I'd already taken my break separately as obviously I wanted to avoid my colleagues. The factory was actually sited on the Thames, with the far end of the building stretching down close to the riverbank. Here the compound was bounded by a corrugated iron fence eight, maybe nine feet, high, and I was never sure whether this was to keep intruders out or to keep the workers in. I'm sure some desperate souls at Cope and Cope must have been tempted at one time or another to try to escape down river or in sheer despair just to throw themselves screaming into the water. The windows in the factory were opaque – God forbid we should glimpse a patch of blue sky for fear it might give us false hopes of freedom – and only the top of the window, which was above head height, opened. This particular day, as I often did when I was on my own, I climbed up onto my workbench and stood up. This way, on a blazing hot day, I could catch the breeze from the river and cool myself down a bit. As I stood there, letting the flow of air from the river caress my neck, I could just see the far side of the river, where couples were strolling hand in hand along the prom, and office workers lazed on the grass enjoying their lunch break. At that moment I knew what a caged bird must feel like. How I longed to be outside toeing a ball about or just flaked out on the riverbank. Then a terrible thought crossed my mind – what if I was destined to always work here – what if I became institutionalised, penned up like one of those battery chickens in this bloody awful sweat box for my entire working life? It could so easily happen. After all it had happened to Norman Fry. Would I end up like him, singing 'As Time Goes By' in a chicken de-beaker factory and surrounded by foul-mouthed part-time prostitutes? At least Norman had had his glory days with Billy Cotton, but my life was only just beginning. As I was having this moment of panic my co-workers returned from lunch, pouring back into the workshop in a big gaggle. They were all nattering excitedly but for once the usual subject of sex had been dropped. Instead of 'the other' they were discussing the other thing that makes the world go round, money. The women were all very happy because the bonus they'd been promised had materialised and they were talking about how they were going to spend it. It was also Friday and everyone was looking forward to the weekend stretching out before them. Apart that is from the two part-time prostitutes, who'd booked a couple of rooms in a hotel in Newbury, handy for the Yanks at Greenham Common. They were the ones who'd be doing the stretching out. I'd jumped quickly down off the workbench when the women had come back in, and was trying to look as though I was busy with something so as not to draw attention, when I heard a cry of excitement. I looked up and saw that one of the women, who'd been going through the large bag of rags that were used for cleaning, had pulled out one particular garment and was holding it up for the others to see. 'You know what, David,' she said with a glint in her eye, 'you haven't been initiated yet.' What she was brandishing to the delight of the whole gang was a romper suit. 'Why don't we strip David off and put these on him instead?' You could've heard a pin drop. They all looked at me. Then two of them started to move, hedging around behind me, the ones in front moving in closer. My heart gave a little thump and I swallowed hard. I was being surrounded. This wasn't just talk – these girls were fired up with end-of-the-week demob fever and they wanted to see some action. In a split second I decided they weren't going to get it from me. I bolted for the door, almost fell down the stairs, then ran out of the building and didn't stop till the factory was out of sight. That night my dad brought my weeks wages home, the princely sum of one pound, nineteen shillings and sixpence (roughly £1.97) and I never went back. I had lasted in my first job just three months. When I'd been given the job Cope and Cope I had told me this would be a trial period. I now realised exactly what they meant by that. I never heard Norman's rendition of 'As Time Goes By' again, but it seemed a small price to pay. It doesn't seem that unusual nowadays for a woman to sue a company for sexual harassment and walk away with £30K just because some guy pinched her arse, or even just made a few lewd remarks. Times have changed. I sometimes wonder how much compensation, if any, I could have got if I'd complained about my female tormentors and taken my case to a tribunal then. I doubt it would have been worth putting that romper suit on for.

The upshot of my escape from Stalag Cope and Cope (we have ways of making you blush) was that I was out of work and needed to get back in it again pretty quick before I became the idle so-and-so of Binfield Heath. What could I do – learning a trade was the smart way to go, but which one? I remembered at school how I'd always looked forward to the woodwork lessons. I just liked working with wood, the feel of it. Taking a sharp chisel to a clean piece of timber was very satisfying; that and watching the grain rising up under the plane. Even the smell of sawn wood had a pleasant effect on me. It smelt like achievement. It seemed logical therefore that I should become a carpenter, well, an apprentice carpenter anyway.

A few of my contemporaries had been awarded apprenticeships with a building firm in Henley-on-Thames, Walden and Son. Perhaps I could follow suit and learn the carpentry trade that way. I managed to arrange an appointment with the managing director of the company Leonard Walden. When I arrived his secretary ushered me into his office, where Mr Walden was sitting behind his desk signing letters. He didn't look up when I entered but just carried on writing. After what seemed an age, though in truth it was probably only three minutes, I coughed just in case he'd forgotten I was there. Still looking down he said, 'Yes, what do you want?' 'I've come to be a carpenter apprentice, sir,' I replied. 'I don't want a carpenter apprentice, I want a bricklaying apprentice; start next Monday, see my secretary on the way out.' What a way to talk to somebody. I didn't like to argue with him though so that was that. A man who hadn't even looked at me, someone who could have met me a minute later and not have recognised me, had just shaped my life for nigh on the next fifty years.

6

When, at the age of fourteen and a bit, I had looked at that form for the youth employment office where it said 'desired occupation', there had been something I wanted to put down. I wanted to write 'professional footballer'. Well it was true. Being a soccer player was the one thing I'd wanted to do, and now aged seventeen it still was really. I was now into the second year of my five years' apprenticeship as a brickie with Walden and Son and had received a call-up to do National Service, but because I was officially indentured in a trade I was granted a deferment. This required me to do my two years' service to queen and country after I'd completed my apprenticeship. As luck would have it, by the time my apprenticeship was over National Service had been abolished so I didn't have to go. I think it would have been a good idea at the time National Service ended if the government had brought in some other way in which young adults could serve their country. For instance, what if everyone, male and female, between the ages of eighteen and twenty were required to give just four donations of blood through the National Blood Service? After all it only takes fifteen minutes to give a donation so one hour spread over two years is not a lot to ask. As a certain JFK once remarked, 'Think not what your country can do for you but what you can do for your country.' We never know when our nearest and dearest might need a transfusion of blood. However I can't see compulsory donations happening now, not with all the 'human rights' issues that would have to be dealt with. By the way, for those that don't know, the indentures were so called because the written apprenticeship agreement between the employer and the apprentice would originally be torn in two, with each party keeping one half till the apprenticeship was completed. The ragged edges of the tear fitted back together like a pair of dentures I suppose, and only the original halves would match up. Not many people know that, as Michael Caine might say. Anyway, my dad had signed the indentures and the apprenticeship meant I didn't go off square-bashing and was instead learning a bloody useful trade, especially with the number of new houses that started going up around that time. In some ways the building apprentices were a source of cheap labour, and I certainly knocked up a few tons of muck over my time. On the other hand the employers did have to send you to college to learn geometry and what have you. Laying bricks is one thing, laying them right is another, and the mysteries of headers and stretchers, common and Flemish bonds all had to be explained. The college release days cost the firms money, and this made them keen to keep you on after your apprenticeship to recoup their investment.

Being a brickie was fair enough, an honest job and all that, but to a kid who can knock a football about a bit and has followed his local club, Reading in my case, since knee-high, there's very often an itch to see if he's got what it takes to be a professional player. I finally decided to stop dreaming about it and take the bull by the horns. Well, I took my bike as a matter of fact, and one Tuesday evening cycled down to the Reading ground at Elm Park to try my luck. The double doors under the stand in Norfolk Road were open, so I wandered in and walked towards the sound of voices further down the corridor. 'Yes son, what do you want?' I turned to face the voice and saw it was none other than the manager, Harry Johnson standing there with a lad who was probably a few years older than me. 'I've come to see if you'll give me a trial sir,' I said. Harry looked me up and down. 'Where do you live?' he asked. I wondered what difference this made to how well I could or couldn't play football, but replied politely, 'Binfield Heath.' He looked thoughtful for a second. 'How did you get here?' 'I cycled.' This seemed to do it for Harry and he said decisively, 'Well, if you've come all that way on a bike you must be keen. All the lads will be here in about an hour.' Harry turned to the lad with him and said, 'Maurice, do me a favour – find some kit for him. You can train with the amateurs.' I was led down the corridor to the kit room. Naively, I asked this lad accompanying me if he too was training with the amateurs. 'No,' he replied, 'I've got to get some treatment for my knee. I picked up a knock on Saturday at Watford.' Maurice was a professional. Maurice Evans turned out to be a great ambassador for Reading, both as a player and an administrator. He died in 2000, at the sadly premature age of just sixty-four. When I attended a memorial service for Maurice in the Madejski Stadium one Sunday evening, my own first memory was of how he'd gone out of his way to help me get kitted out on amateur night all those years ago. A commemorative plaque has been erected at the stadium describing Maurice as a player, a manager and a gentleman. That summed the guy up exactly.

At that time Reading had four teams. Their first team played in Division Three (south), the reserves competed in the Combination and the 'A side' played in the Hampshire League. Lastly there were the under-eighteens who played in the Reading and District Minor League. This youth tournament was regularly won over several years by one of two teams, either the Reading or Battle minors. My keenness in cycling from Binfield Heath to the ground that Tuesday night seemed to have impressed Harry Johnson, and so my 'career' with Reading kicked off. The amateurs trained on Tuesdays and Thursdays, but after a couple of weeks I realised the training consisted of three things – running, running and yet more running. We just didn't get near a ball during the week at all. The philosophy behind this was that if we hadn't kicked the ball for seven days, then by Saturday we'd be hungry for it and play a far better game. What a load of crap!

During this period my football skills didn't improve but I don't think I've ever been fitter. What with working on a building site all week, cycling back and forth to the Elm Park ground twice a week and running round and round that bloody track like some demented greyhound I'd have to be. It was like doing a permanent triathlon. Several times running round the track on the perimeter of the pitch I lost my dinner after three or four laps, so I gave up eating before training and used to call in at the chippy on the way home to stoke up. If it's really true that 'you are what you eat' then during my time with the Reading minors I was a battered 'cod and large chips please mate'. Not forgetting the salt and vinegar and the newsprint off the wrapping. Alf Tupper, 'the Tough of the Track', could have been modelled on me. Alf was a comic-strip character who split his time between his car repair business under a railway arch and winning medals on the athletics track. He always seemed to be hastily slipping out of his overalls and into his running spikes, arriving at the starting block just as the gun went off. After a hard day's welding he was nevertheless usually first to breast the tape and all he ever ate was fish and chips. Substitute bricklaying for car repairs and me and Alf were two of a kind. Oh, except that he was a champ in his chosen sporting field. I still had to prove myself.

The minors were run by a guy called Paddy. I never did know his proper name, but he was extremely fit and to my knowledge no one ever crossed him. The minors played many of their home games at Prospect Park, a public recreation ground across the road from Elm Park, so we'd get changed at the club and walk across to our allotted pitch. One particular Saturday early in the season, Paddy got to the pitch and discovered he'd left the team's water behind. The weather being extremely hot it was important for the players to have a regular intake of fluids to combat the effects of dehydration. During a break in play in the game the players would run to the touchline to take water on board from the trainer. So this particular day he walks across to the gents' toilet in the park, only to find the top of the tap had been removed to prevent it being left on by mistake. Now I was only a reserve (this was before substitutes were allowed, thank goodness for me as it turned out that day) and Paddy calls me over to the gents, explains the situation and tells me what we're going to do. 'Come in here,' he says. I follow him into the toilet cubicle. 'Right,' he says, 'when I say go, you flush the toilet and I'll catch some water in this.' I looked at what Paddy was holding. It was the inner tube of an old football, which had been cut open. Fair enough, if the players are hot and bothered they're not going to complain so long as the water that cools them down is wet. Beggars can't be choosers and all that. I did wonder though if Paddy was going to explain this to the players. I assumed he wasn't going to let them actually drink it, or was he? Anyway Paddy crouches round the pan, positions the inner tube and I tug on the chain. Whoosh! It was a good flush, as flushes go, with more than enough water coming down to prevent eleven men getting heat stroke for ninety minutes. Trouble is, hardly any went into the inner tube. Now, anyone who's ever had to use a public convenience knows they're not always the cleanest of places, especially the bit you sat down and do your business on. These municipal bogs in Prospect Park were no exception. Particularly the bit you sit down on, which Paddy was looking down into at that moment. Which is why when Paddy did what he did next, I had to look away. He leans forward again, dips the inner tube into the water at the bottom of the toilet bowl and starts bailing it up into the inner tube. Trying to catch water from the cistern was bad enough; this made my stomach churn. Mind you, it was effective. Paddy had soon filled his water bucket and we made our way back to the match. They were now about twenty minutes into the first half and with the temperature rising, you could see the effects of the heat on the players. Soon they were less interested in winning the ball than fighting for a few swigs from Paddy's water bucket. They say if you could see what goes on in most restaurant kitchens you'd never eat or drink there, and this theory has always reminded me of that match in Prospect Park. As the water from Paddy's sponge coursed into the thirsty mouths of my team mates I kept picturing where it had been lying only minutes earlier. In the second half three of the team were violently sick. Paddy told them sympathetically that 'heat can do that', and who was I to dispute the great man's wisdom. I was only a reserve, thank God.

I thoroughly enjoyed my game and knew I could play a bit, but even with the arrogance of youth I realised there were many lads of my age at the club with far more skill than me. It wasn't exactly a surprise therefore when at the end of the season I got a letter from Reading thanking me for my services and telling me I was free to sign for any other club if I wished. In other words, bugger off and don't come back. There was a shade of disappointment at the time naturally, but looking back I'm glad I made that stab at going professional. I'd hate to have got to the age I am now and always be wondering if I could have made it onto my field of dreams. At least I got it out of my system and my life could move on. My advice today to any youngster is to follow your dreams and ambitions. You never know, they might come true. If not, well, no one goes through life without some failures and you learn a lot in the process.

Though professional football may have given up on me, I wasn't going to give up on football. I went on to spend several years playing for various junior- and intermediate-level clubs until one season, when I was in my early thirties, I suffered the classic footballer's injury of a torn cartilage. That and the youngsters who were now beginning to run rings round me on the pitch made me realise that age was catching up on me. As everyone discovers, I was not Peter Pan after all. Besides I now felt there were better things for a man to do at the weekend than stand around in a field, especially on a freezing January afternoon when the ground is like iron and your only consoling thought is that you're not a brass monkey. So what was I going to do with my spare time now? Some men take up golf, but to me golf is a just a way of spoiling a good walk. If I needed that level of excitement I could always paint a wall and watch it dry. After the cartilage operation I knew I had to continue my involvement in football in some way, and although it was a young man's sport on the pitch, there were plenty of other ways to stay in touch with the game. Refereeing was one option, but referees are a bit like traffic wardens with shorts and a whistle, or tax inspectors: nobody likes them Although I've never wanted to be liked by everybody, I didn't want to be hated by everybody either. Refereeing just wasn't for me. There is however another job in football that can seem a bit like being a referee and that is the position of club secretary. It is my firm opinion that if a stranger walked into a small community and asked to be directed to the village idiot, they would be escorted directly to the door of the local football club secretary. Quite frankly the job is not worth a bucket of spit. In almost all clubs, the actual work is carried out by a few dedicated members while the hangers-on do nothing but whinge, complain and moan about everything. And who takes the brunt of all this? You've guessed it, the club secretary. Nevertheless a club secretary is what I became, and having said all that there were a few lighter moments. At one place I was at, a guy who had been associated with the club for many years sadly died. In his will he had made a request to be cremated and for his ashes to be scattered in the centre circle. Now during my time at this club the deceased had been one of the aforementioned whingers and moaners, forever finding fault with this, that and the other. As club secretary the bloke had been the bane of my life. But now he'd whinged his last, and was on his way to that great football stadium in the sky. No one speaks ill of the dead and the least we could all do was give him a good send-off in the manner of his choosing. So one Sunday shortly after the funeral the club committee met up with the man's family on the pitch. It had been agreed we would do the whole thing properly so we all dressed in our club blazers and positioned ourselves in formation around the centre circle, bowed our heads and listened while the club chaplain delivered some well chosen prayers. I can't recall the words exactly, and I don't think he could find any passages in the Bible that related to football (a book of two halves?), but the family looked suitably moved. With the prayers concluded the chaplain lifts the urn high and slowly and begins ceremoniously to broadcast the ashes. It was a fairly breezy day and without thinking I had taken up a position down-wind of the chaplain. As the ashes tumbled forth the breeze quickly took hold and carried them across to where I was standing. We all still had our heads lowered with hands clasped in front, like a penalty shoot-out. I wriggled my nose as the first few bits tickled my face. I was itching to sidestep the slipstream of the loved one's remains but with the stillness and dignity of everyone else present, particularly the guy's family, it wouldn't have looked right. I remained rooted to the spot as the drifting ash found its way into my eyes, making them smart and sting. Before long tears were forming and trickling down my face. After the ceremony I felt a hand on my shoulder. It was one of the relatives. 'If you don't mind my saying so,' she said, 'I noticed how upset you were. He must have meant a lot to you.' Dabbing my eyes with a handkerchief, I nodded. I didn't tell her that in life the bloke had perpetually got right up my nose, and had now proved he could be just as bloody irritating dead.

The last club for which I was secretary was Abingdon Town, which at that time played in the Isthmian League. Two or three times a season all the clubs in this league would be summoned to a meeting. The organisers took these meetings seriously. So seriously in fact that any club failing to send a representative would be fined some ridiculous amount of money for non-attendance. As secretary of Abingdon Town, it was my job to go to these league meetings. On the allotted days I would knock off work early, catch a rush-hour train from Didcot Parkway to Paddington and then jump in a taxi that dropped me outside the Hilton Hotel in Park Lane. One particular night I'd just climbed out of the taxi and was settling up with the cabbie when I felt someone pulling my sleeve. Since I was now in the wicked city, the 'smoke', I span round instinctively thinking I was about to be mugged. Silly really, as I was only a few yards from the hotel foyer and there were plenty of people around apart from the cabbie and the doorman in his top hat and tailcoat, though you can never tell. Actually I should have realised I wasn't being confronted by some young thug even before I turned round. It was the smell. I'm not an expert on perfume but I know it's usually only worn by women, in this case a very attractive young lady who stood there, still gripping my sleeve and looking pleadingly into my eyes. She was tall, slim and beautiful and dressed to kill. Somehow I knew she wasn't from the Isthmian Football League. 'Listen, I'm ever so sorry to bother you but …' At this point I almost thought she was going to ask if I could spare some change, but no, the designer clothes she had on meant it was more likely to be me asking her for a hand-out. Meanwhile she was eyeing the doorman a bit nervously. 'Yes love?' I said. 'Well, it's like this,' she went on. 'I've arranged to meet someone in the hotel, but they won't let me go in on my own.' I looked over at the doorman who had just closed the door of a Roller and pocketed a tip. He was now vigilantly patrolling the hotel entrance again. The penny dropped. 'Well …' I began. 'I'll give you twenty quid if you'll just go in with me as far as the lift,' she said. Twenty quid, hmm, being a gentleman I could hardly refuse such a damsel in distress. 'All right,' I shrugged. She smiled sweetly, pressed a twenty-pound note into my hand, and arm in arm we passed through the big revolving doors and into the palatial surroundings of the Hilton Hotel. Crossing the sumptuous foyer I looked around to see if any of my colleagues from the Isthmian League were there, but I didn't recognise anyone among the businessmen and tourists reclining in the leather sofas. When we got to the lift my nameless companion whispered a quick thank you, then vanished behind the shiny, silently gliding doors. Later on that evening, sitting in the boring and long-winded league meeting, the thought crossed my mind that if the building trade ever went slack I could always nip up to the smoke and make a few bob living off immoral earnings – sorry, escorting young ladies to hotels. It had only taken me half a minute to walk the girl from the cab to the lift. Twenty quid for half a minute's work, now how much was that an hour … I wonder if she wrote off my fee against tax?

After getting the football club secretary bit out of my system, I decided to follow Reading seriously. Up till then as a spectator I'd always stood in the open, up at the Tilehurst end of the ground, but the purchase of a season ticket entitled me to use the 'posh' seats under cover in the main stand. This was an upgrade – in theory. The turnstile to the stand was in Norfolk Road, and at the bottom of the wooden steps leading up to the tiered seats was the gents' toilet. This 'convenience' was in truth an evil-smelling place, which even the most desperate of fans would think twice about visiting. Located at the very top of the steps, spectators could partake of sustenance at the ground's prestigious restaurant facilities – i.e. the burger bar. Among my most potent memories of Elm Park are of being halfway up those steps as the smell of frying onions wafted down to meet the stench of stale urine from the gents' toilet. If this knockout cocktail could have been bottled and pumped through the air vents of the visiting teams' dressing room, I firmly believe

Reading would never have been defeated at home. Tony Blair got the wrong part of the globe over weapons of mass destruction. If he'd inhaled during any home game at Elm Park he'd have realised that.

On Sunday, 3 May 1998 Reading played their last league game at Elm Park, with Norwich City the victorious visitors. The game epitomised the whole season, which had been one of tedious mediocrity. We had finished rock bottom of Division 1 and were duly relegated. Rusting, ramshackle Elm Park was quite frankly not fit for purpose. The same could be said for quite a number of the players whom manager Tommy Burns had brought to the club. Chairman John Madejski would be leading us to the Promised Land – a 24,000 all-seater stadium just off the M4. The first league game against Luton Town which we won 3–1 was, on reflection, a false dawn. By mid September, I'm ashamed to say I had more points on my driving licence (nine) than the team had struggled to gain in the league. The team just did not do justice to the palatial surroundings of the Madejski Stadium. Indeed it wasn't until Tommy left and headed back over Hadrian's Wall that the club began to show its true potential. Even now as I sit in my seat in the west upper stand I find it difficult to believe that 'my team' plays here. One thing I had been told about the Madejski Stadium was that piles had been driven deep into the ground so that when Reading reached the Premiership the ground could be extended. As we were in Division 2 at the time I never mentioned this fact to anyone in case men in white coats came and carted me away. But lo and behold, here we are in our second season in the Premiership, having finished in the top half in the first season, and hoping to overcome the dreaded second season syndrome. And planning permission has been granted for work to commence on enlarging the stadium capacity to 37,000. Now how does the song go – if you don't have a dream, how you gonna have a dream come true ...

7

When I was a teenager Thursday nights were always a bit special. Not only was it the day I got paid but there were also the delights of the Henley Jazz Club to look forward to. I don't think though that I ever heard any jazz as such played at the club, and I doubt if Humphrey Littleton ever featured on the bill. Instead, the 'music' was generally provided by some local wannabe rock and roll outfit, who, inspired by the big stars and all hoping to be the next Elvis or Cliff Richard, would get up on stage and crash away for all they were worth. But to be honest the music wasn't the main attraction for most of the youthful clientele. Every Thursday night, together with a friend, Geoff Burt, I would catch a bus down to Henley-on-Thames. We were two seventeen-year-olds with money in our pockets and our faces covered in adolescent spots. Testosterone was bursting out of our pores. Bugger the music – we were looking for girls.

In the early sixties all the girls seemed to wear a type of skirt that made them look like lampshades on legs. If you can remember this particular item of female fashion you're probably reading this tucked up in an old folks' home. For those who have no idea what they were like, picture basically a very full skirt, gathered tight at the girl's waist. Underneath the skirt would be worn a waist petticoat. A seam was sewn all around this petticoat about three inches from the bottom edge, and into the seam a length of bone was inserted. This made the skirt billow out all round, resembling, as I say, a lampshade. Quite often, when a girl sat down in one of these skirts, if she wasn't careful her skirt would do its own thing and spring up in front of her, showing her knickers and suspenders. (I wonder if suspenders will ever come back into fashion?)

Anyway, one Thursday night, Geoff and I arrived at the club as usual to check out the 'talent' and saw, in the middle of the dance floor, these two lampshades, whirling and twirling to the music. They appeared to be friends. The racket from the wannabes that night was particularly deafening. My testosterone-fuelled mate shouted to me over the din: 'Come on, let's split those two up – I'll take the one on the right and you can dance with the other one.' The 'other one' was a fifteen-year-old girl called Julie Hales. She and I seemed to hit it off right away, and from that night we began to see each other on a regular basis.

Julie lived in the centre of Henley, above the bakery and shop owned and run by her father. It was situated less than

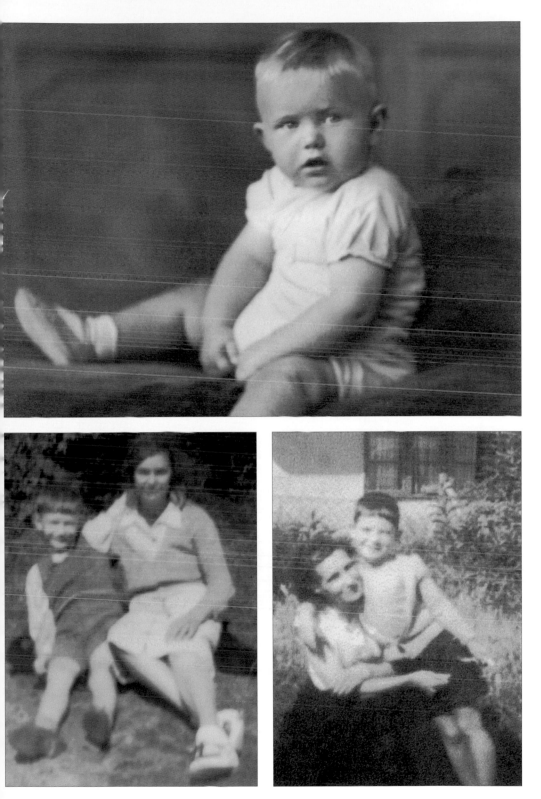

Above: Me as a toddler.

Below left and right: Parallel lives. On the left, I sit with my adopted mother, Rose Sharp, while on the right my brother Ian sits with our shared, natural mother, Rose McEwan.

Above left: A proud prefect, aged 15.

Above right: Sat with pencil in hand, 1954.

Below: In a more comfortable seat, alongside my teammates in Rotherfield Grays Secondary School's football team (I'm second from right, bottom row).

Above: Julie and I on our wedding day and *left*, the author as a young man.

Two contrasting faces of fatherhood. *Above left*: Sergeant Major David McEwan, mine and Ian's father, and *above right*, my Dad, Percy Sharp.

Below: Rose Wort, as she was then, in 1940, two years before she was to give birth to me.

half a mile from Henley Bridge, in the market place, which is called now Falaise Square. (Why they changed the name to a French one I don't know, perhaps it was something to do with town twinning, *entente cordiale* or going into the Common Market.) I remember the first time I visited Julie's home being struck by how large the rooms were. The 'blue' room, which was the family room, had a large open fireplace, which though a welcoming, cosy sight was still much too small to heat the whole room. This meant that on cold days everyone used to crowd close to the fire. If you were one of the first to enter the room you could pick the seat nearest the hearth, bearing in mind however that Julie's dad always occupied the same chair in the same space – next to his pipe rack and books and closest to the fire – and woe betide you if you sat in that chair. Julie's mum usually sat on the other side of the fireplace, often having a rug wrapped round her for extra warmth. Anyone else who was using the room would pull up one of the old lumpy armchairs and try to warm their hands and feet by stretching them out towards the glowing coals. The other main room was called the drawing room – why it was called this I do not know, since no one 'withdrew' to it exactly; it was just a customary name I suppose. The drawing room was used for entertaining guests, and like the family room was huge. It contained a piano, a radiogram, a large bookcase and a massive round table. There was also a large settee, on which Julie's dad would take an afternoon nap following his very early morning start in the bakery, and several armchairs. There were three large windows overlooking the market place, from which you could look down on the general hustle and bustle. The drawing room had the additional luxury of a gas fire.

To the rear of the property was a spacious kitchen with vast wooden dressers, on which were arranged the china cups, saucers and plates. In the centre of the kitchen stood a very large table where Julie's family would gather together to eat three regular meals a day, breakfast, dinner and tea, with nothing in between. At teatime there was always bread and butter, jam and cakes and cups of tea. The floor of the kitchen was laid with enormous flagstones which were always cold. They were also extremely difficult to keep clean and needed regular attention. I recall visiting one day to find Mrs Lidgley the cleaner yet again washing the floor, down on her hands and knees with a metal bucket filled with hot soapy water beside her. Mrs Lidgley was as broad as she was high, and while scrubbing the flagstones her more than ample body would sway vigorously from side to side, showing to all the world her pink apple-catchers (very large ladies' knickers with elastic at each leg, which covered virtually the whole of the thigh down to the knee) – what a sight, and ample room for a good few pounds of Bramleys! The scullery was where the washing up was done, in an old stone sink with a wooden draining board. The scullery also housed a built-in copper that was used to heat water. I recall Julie telling me that there was a washing machine, not of the hi-tech type that most people have today, nor even a twin tub, but one that had to be filled manually with hot water.

On the top of the removable lid was a handle and on the underside a paddle–type utensil. Whoever did the washing – usually Julie's mum I imagine – had to stand over the machine and literally keep turning the handle on the lid, which would move the paddle within the tub and pulsate the washing. Remember how these appliances were called 'labour-saving' and intended to lighten the housewife's chores? It was a step up from bashing the clothes on the riverbank, but still hard work I should think. The items that got washed first were those that could withstand very hot water, usually the cotton sheets and pillowcases, followed by the more delicate garments, then finally the dark wash. After each batch had been 'machine washed' they were passed through a hand wringer – a mangle consisting of two rollers set close together which would be turned by a handle to squeeze out the excess water – and into a large container of clean water for the 'rinse cycle'. Then the washing was put back through the mangle again and hung out on the line to dry. Monday was always washing and housecleaning day; Tuesday was always ironing day; and I suppose you just had to hope for good drying weather on the Monday.

To the rear of the scullery was the bake house where all the bread and cakes were made. The bake house was the size of a small village hall, with red quarry tiles on the floor and a stone sink with a single tap where all the baking utensils were washed up. On each side of the room were wooden worktops and to one side a large dough-mixing machine. Once the dough had been made it was transferred to a large wooden worktop in the centre of the room to be kneaded and rolled by hand before being put into tins of various shapes and sizes to make cottage, tin, sandwich and bolster loaves. Suspended over the central worktop hung the peels – very long-handled wooden tools, rather like rowing oars or paddles, which were used to take the loaves in and out of the huge oil-fired ovens. When the bread was sufficiently cool each loaf would be removed from its tin, placed on a wooden baker's tray and carried into the shop. The bread flour was stored in hessian sacks in the loft above the bake house. When more flour was required the baker would ascend to the loft and let down a chute, which would replenish the flour bin below. The yeast was of course purchased in bulk, and came in large square lumps, which were kept down in the cold, dark cellar. The baking of the bread was all done by Julie's dad, and he employed a gentleman called Mr Tappin to produce the confectionary. Mr Tappin used to make some wonderful cakes – Eccles, marble, sponge, fruit, meringues, iced fancies, macaroons, eclairs, doughnuts and all kinds of buns. Also popular then were 'traffic lights', a type of shortbread with three small round hollows filled with red, orange and green jam. Special orders were taken for birthday and other celebratory cakes, for which Mr Tappin's superb icing skills were renowned, creating the most intricate designs using only a simple piping bag that he would fashion from a piece of greaseproof paper.

At the counter the loaves would be wrapped in a type of

tissue paper and handed to the customer, who would then place their purchase carefully in their basket. You could also buy sweets by the quarter pound. These were displayed colourfully and tantalisingly in large glass jars with screw-top lids – sherbet lemons, aniseed twist, mint toffees, glacé mints. To the other side of the shop was a cafe where, after shopping and before catching the buses home, people would gather to catch up on the gossip, have a freshly made pot of tea or coffee and perhaps a scone and butter or one of the freshly baked cakes. An especially busy time for the business was during the Henley Regatta week, usually spread over the last days of June and early July. A lot of college rowing teams from America and elsewhere, many sporting pink leander ties and blazers with all the subtlety of seaside deckchairs, would descend on the town at this time. Those teams that got knocked out in the first races would often have to wait several days for a flight home, and could be seen drowning their sorrows and staggering around the town. The other visitors to Henley at this time were the hordes of spectators. These tended to be equally parched, but not being dejected at their failure to win any cups, were happy enough with non-alcoholic refreshment. These day-trippers generally had a lot of money to spend, and would swarm in to the Hales' cafe to slake their thirst and replenish themselves, ordering afternoon tea, consisting of a pot of tea, bread, butter and jam and a selection of cakes, all for around two shillings and sixpence in old money – the equivalent of about twelve-and-a-half new pence. The atmosphere in

Henley during the Regatta was always buzzing, and the bakery cafe so popular that additional staff would be employed to cope with the demand.

I had been going out with Julie for several months and everything was going well, apart, that is, from one dark cloud on the horizon. I had still not told her about Mum and Dad not being my biological parents. Looking back, my emotions at the time swung between embarrassment and shame, which I suppose are one and the same thing. The fact was that I hadn't spoken to anyone about the matter since that awful evening four years earlier when my parents had told me I wasn't theirs. After the emotional dust had settled I had just pushed the matter further and further to the back of my mind. Undoubtedly, the raw pain of that occasion, and the negative way my mum and dad seemed to feel about the way they had brought me into their lives, had haunted my own thoughts. Of course at this time I still had no idea even how or where they had obtained me; whether they'd selected me from an orphanage or made some other arrangement I had no idea. Whatever route it was that I had travelled to arrive at 1, Spring Terrace, my parents seemed intensely fearful of discussing it. Perhaps it was simply that deep down, or not so deep down, my mum in particular had felt an incurable sorrow that she could never be fully a 'proper' mother to her son, and regarded herself as a kind of fraud and a failure with regard to me. That scene in the kitchen, with my mum sobbing as my dad grimly handed me the birth certificate was not the kind of thing I wanted to go through ever again.

I couldn't approach Mum and Dad to talk things over, since I knew it would only make them unhappy and I simply couldn't bear the sight of Mum crying again.

Maybe I was in denial about the whole situation. I was now coming up to eighteen, and with regard to telling Julie I suppose in some ways I was building the issue out of all proportion to what it actually was. The longer we went out together without my telling her, the larger it all loomed in my mind, and the harder it seemed to just come out casually with the information that, 'Oh, by the way, Mum and Dad aren't my natural parents.' If I'd told her on our first meeting she might have thought it odd, that I was obsessed with the matter. But now she might well wonder why I hadn't mentioned it before! When is the right time for that kind of announcement, and how exactly are you supposed to phrase it? I know it sounds stupid now, but the more I put off telling Julie about my past, the bigger the problem became.

One day I had an idea. I would enlist the help of Julie's parents. I figured that if I told them first about my 'adoption', it would be, if you like, a halfway house to telling Julie. So one evening I arrived earlier than usual at the Hales' home, knowing full well that Julie would not yet be ready for us to go out for the evening, and I'd therefore have time to talk to her parents on their own. As usual Mr and Mrs Hales were installed in the family room, relaxing after their day's toil in the bakery. They invited me to sit down, and after all the usual small talk, I just waded in with what I had to say, telling them in the process virtually everything I knew about myself, and what I didn't know – i.e. who my biological parents were. When I had finished unburdening myself Julie's dad looked thoughtful, chewing heavily on the stem of his pipe. After a moment he removed the pipe from his mouth and said to me, 'You're coming up to eighteen. Now, in all those years how many times have you been really hungry – how many times have you not had decent clothes on your back?' I looked at him and shook my head. 'Never,' I said. 'So,' went on Mr Hales, 'the Sharps have given you a good start. It doesn't matter at your age about your past, it's where you're going in the future that should be occupying your mind right now.' Well, I thought, so far so good. But who was going to tell Julie all this? Mr Hales then went on to explain to me how if I wished, I could change my name from Wort to Sharp by something called 'statutory declaration'. All I had to do, he said, was go to a solicitor and swear an oath on the Bible, and that would be that. At this point, Julie's mum, who so far hadn't uttered a word, chipped in by saying, 'I think in all fairness to Julie you should tell her what you've told us, but we don't mind in the least about your past.' By now I couldn't believe how relaxed they both were about the whole thing. At that moment Julie herself walked into the room. She seemed to sense that a discussion had been taking place. 'What have you all been talking about?' she asked. 'Nothing much,' I said casually, knowing I wasn't fooling her for a minute. Julie looked at her mum, then her dad, who coughed hurriedly, putting his pipe back in his mouth and burying his head in his newspaper. As soon as we were out of the house and walking down the street I said to Julie, 'I've got something important to tell you.' She glanced at me. 'Oh, what?' she said. I paused. Telling her mum and dad had been so surprisingly easy. I thought, suppose Julie has more of a problem with it? Dragging my feet on the pavement I said awkwardly, 'Well, it's like this, you see, it's my parents, they're not … my real parents.' 'What do you mean, not your real parents?' replied Julie. 'Well, I'm sort of adopted,' I said. We both stopped walking and Julie looked at me for what seemed like an age. She then said, 'So am I.' I stared at her. I asked her to repeat what she'd said, which she did. 'You're adopted too?' I said. 'Yes.' I just couldn't believe it. All the months I'd spent worrying about telling her and lo and behold, hers was a similar story. Hand in hand we strolled out into the town, while Julie told me how she'd spent the first few years of her life in a children's home in Banbury, Oxfordshire. When she was five Mr and Mrs Hales had officially adopted her. Julie said that from the outset she had known the Hales were her adoptive parents, and thus she didn't really have any emotional baggage, with things being out in the open. I thought no wonder her mum and dad had been so laid-back about my own story just now.

Apart from the fact we liked each other, the knowledge that we'd both had a less than ideal start to our lives seemed to give Julie and me an additional bond, and five years after meeting in the Henley Jazz Club we got married. And amazingly enough her friend, 'the one on the right' that night in the club, Jackie Street, married my mate Geoff Burt six weeks before our wedding, with Geoff and I each being the other's best man.

8

'And they're off to a flying start …!' The swinging sixties
that was; I don't think anyone called them that at the
time, and life didn't seem noticeably different in 1960 from
how it had been before. By the end of the year though there
were a few changes. For those who liked a flutter, off-course
gambling was made legal in Britain, and so instead of the
unofficial bookie or runner who'd take bets on the building
site or the factory, betting shops started springing up in the
high streets. The legislation also enabled the big bingo firms
to get in on the act, taking over many of the old church halls
and cinemas to accommodate armies of mainly women for
their regular nights out of 'eyes down', socialising and
spending. As someone said about commercial telly, the
deregulation of gaming that year must have been a licence to
print money, and now we're seeing it happen all over again
with the new casinos opening up. The 'feel-good' event of

1960 was Princess Margaret's wedding to Anthony Armstrong-Jones, Lord Snowden as he became better known. 'Good Luck and Every Happiness' proclaimed the front-page headline of the *Daily Herald* on 6 May as 'singing, cheering crowds jammed the streets of London this morning ...'

But Princess Margaret wasn't the only one to change her name that year. 'That'll be one pound four shillings and sixpence please,' said the clerk. I was in the outer office of 'Collins, Dryland and Thorowgood', solicitors of Henley-on-Thames. It seemed a lot for a small bit of paper but to me it was worth it. I went into the office as Stewart David Wort, and came out as David Stuart Sharp. My mum and Dad had changed my Christian names around, and altered the spelling, a bit like putting their fingerprints on me I suppose. I hadn't told anyone I was going to make my name legal that day in August 1960. Why had I decided to do it at last? Maybe it was hearing Elvis singing 'It's Now or Never' on the radio. Of course everyone knew me as Dave Sharp, but now entering adulthood there were times when it was awkward to have a birth certificate that read differently. Not that I'd yet obtained a new birth certificate. What I had just done was change my name to Sharp by what they called statutory declaration, as Julie's parents had advised me I could if I wanted. I was no longer a Wort. I knew my mum and dad would be pleased I'd done it off my own bat, and when I got home and told them I found I wasn't wrong. They didn't say much of course, but the look on their faces was enough, especially my mum's. I did wonder, not for the first time, about the Worts, my 'real' parents. What sort of people were they and why had they got rid of me? The war had been on of course and that may have had something to do with it. Were they still alive? This was the weird part of the whole thing – the idea that they might be walking around somewhere, and if they were local that they might have passed me by in the street. Maybe they knew who I was and kept an eye on me. Weirder still was the possibility that I might have seen them. What would they say if we suddenly came face to face? I wondered how much my mum and dad knew that they hadn't told me. Since that dreadful night they'd shown me the birth certificate the subject had, as I said, been taboo in the house, and there was no way I wanted to cause an upset by asking questions. I was now Dave Sharp in the letter of the law as well, my mum and dad's only son and proud of it. We were a happy family and sleeping dogs would have to lie.

Breakfast was always something that I took for granted at Spring Terrace. While still at school I knew as certain as the rising of the sun that mum would have tea, toast and cereal and sometimes something cooked waiting for me when I returned from my paper round, and ever since I'd started work she'd been getting up earlier to prepare everything before I set off. Come rain or shine breakfast was always on the table. Then one morning it wasn't. As I went down the stairs I heard Mum's voice calling from her room. 'Is that you, David? Sorry there's nothing on the table, love. I feel like a bit of a lay-in this morning. You help yourself will you? There should be a fresh pint of milk …' I didn't think much of it at the time but looking back I suppose that day was the start of her illness. The lay-in became the norm and she was never up now before I left for work. Then one day I returned home early because we'd been rained off and Mum had gone back to bed for a nap. This happened again a number of times. Gradually I got used to the idea that something had shifted, that she was different. Day by day, almost imperceptibly her features were changing, but when you see someone regularly it is harder to notice any alteration in them. There was a general assumption that Mum was 'under the weather' and her condition remained for me on this rather vague, manageable level. The fact she was actually ill just didn't sink in, partly perhaps because she simply wouldn't have the doctor call at the house, and of course being anxious about going out she wouldn't allow anyone to take her to the surgery. This was something I used to hear my dad pleading with her about. Then one day I returned to find Dad preparing the dinner. 'Come in son, it's nearly ready, sit down.' I said, 'Whose is that car outside?' 'It's the doctor's. He's up with your mum now. There, you eat up – I'll be in the front room with the doctor.' It had been Dad who'd finally sought medical help against my mother's wishes, and that night after an examination she was told what she'd been dreading, that she needed to be admitted to the Royal Berkshire Hospital in Reading. An ambulance arrived that night and as she was brought downstairs I realised for the first time how bad she looked, her face puffy and misshapen, and with a strange pallor.

At this time I was just seven months short of my twenty-first birthday and in the last year of my bricklaying apprenticeship. The one fortunate thing was that I was working in Reading, and so the following night, as soon as I had knocked off, I jumped into my little Standard Eight car and drove straight to the hospital. Mum gave a little smile when she saw me. Looking round at the other beds where there were vases of flowers and cards I felt guilty I hadn't brought anything; I'd just wanted to get to see her as quickly as possible. The nurses had drained a lot of fluid from her and she actually looked a lot better. I bent over and kissed her on the forehead. 'How you feeling Mum?' I said. 'Oh, not too bad dear, how's your work going?' 'All right, all right.' 'You must be hungry after being out on that scaffolding all day. Make sure you get plenty to eat tonight, won't you. Is Dad cooking a hot meal?' 'Hmm, yeah – yeah, I think so.' Suddenly I felt tongue-tied with my own mum. 'Dad says he'll be in later.' She nodded and took my hand, which I realised was coarse and hard from using the mortar. Her own hand felt very small and delicate in it. 'Soon be home Mum,' I said.

Wednesday, 15 May 1963 was to be a special day, and the sports pages of the papers were full of it. If Tottenham Hotspur could defeat Atletico Madrid they would become the first British club to win a European trophy, and even without the injured and inspirational Dave Mackay everyone thought they stood a good chance. Dad had visited the hospital straight from work, where Mum had assured him she was feeling fine and that he should get home to enjoy the match on the radio with me. I had already looked in earlier, only for her to wave me off after a quarter of an hour with a similar instruction. She was still gently waving as I looked back from the door of the hospital ward. By the time Dad arrived and had put his bike in the woodshed I had dinner on the table. The prognosis was good. Mum was getting better and would be coming home. Before long everything would be back to normal. In the meantime, tonight Dad and I had football to listen to. At that time outside broadcasts were transmitted on the Home Service and the reception, particularly from overseas, tended to fade in and out without warning. Tonight's match was coming live from Rotterdam so after we'd cleared away the dinner things we both sat down next to the radio ready to retune the frequency at the first wow and flutter of interference. Not long after kick-off Jimmy Greaves had just put Spurs in front when the commentary began to drift off and the strident tones of some unrecognisable foreign language came over the airwaves. We both reached for the radio. 'No, let me do it,' said my dad, and like a safecracker attempting to open a complex combination lock he pressed his ear close to the fabric covering of the speaker and very slowly turned the tuning knob. The little arrow inched along the waveband – Light, Hilversum, Warsaw, other voices came drifting in and out, English,

American, what sounded like German. Then for a few seconds the reception oscillated between a classical concert and a pop programme – 'Beethoven's Fifth is perhaps one of the best-known ... and at number three it's Gerry and the Pacemakers with "You'll Never Walk Alone" ...' The radio then gave an undulating whistle as the match broadcast came through loud and clear only to break up again in a crackle of East European accents. 'Here, let me have a go, Dad,' I said. 'No, it's alright, I've got it, no, it's gone again – now who's that at this time of night?' The knock on the door had startled both of us. 'I'll get it,' I said. I opened the door and saw Mr Williams, our neighbour from a few doors down. 'Is your dad in David?' he said. 'There's been a phone call.' We didn't have a telephone and had given Mr Williams' number to the hospital in case they needed to contact us. 'Is it about Mum?' I asked. By now Dad had joined me at the door. The radio was giving off just a low buzzing sound now. 'Percy, the hospital just called; Rose has passed away. I'm sorry.' Suddenly the radio burst back into life: 'And John White has added a second for Spurs!' The commentator's voice was almost drowned out by the roar of the crowd, cheering and chanting, whistling and whooping. 'What an atmosphere!' I went back over to the sideboard and turned the set off. Dad didn't say anything, just walked to his chair and slumped into it. The occasion on which father and son had been sharing a mutual sporting interest, in the expectation that the person they loved most in the world would soon return, had turned into the worst night of their lives.

Overnight Dad seemed to get physically smaller, already withdrawing deep into his personal grief. Apart from her stay in hospital he and Mum had rarely been far from each other's side. Now after twenty-nine years death had parted them. Mum had only been fifty-two years old. What had happened to the good prognosis? Cancer is unpredictable and there can be few families that are not touched by it. (I don't think Dad ever fully recovered from my mum's death.)

The next day the May sunshine was dazzling. I hadn't really slept and went out in the very early morning to call on a friend that I worked with. I told him about my mum, adding, 'So I won't be going in today, if you could let the firm know.' He seemed embarrassed and just turned away. 'OK,' he said. By the time I got back to the house my dad was completely broken up. I don't think he knew what to do, and I didn't either. We both just sat there staring into space for a long time. I looked at the radio, which was still tuned to the Home Service, and heard again in my head the roar from the stadium that had come just after Mr Williams' announcement. Spurs had won 5–1. The fans and the nation were in jubilant mood. I made a pot of tea but neither of us could eat anything. After a couple of hours, like most people do I suppose, we put ourselves on automatic pilot and set out to tackle the practicalities of the situation we found ourselves in. Like robots we dragged ourselves out of the front door and into my car. We needed to go into Reading first to the hospital, where just a few hours before my mum had waved and smiled at me from her bed. We had to obtain a notification of death in those days, before seeing the Registrar who would issue the death certificate. Last stop was the undertakers to arrange the funeral. Each of these visits felt like another stab wound, as every briskly sympathetic official turned the knife one more excruciating time, each form and signature and well-meaning word plunging the blade deeper into my heart.

The following day Dad and I both went into work, him to Cope and Cope, me to Walden's. This abrupt return wasn't through necessity. I suppose we both needed to reach for some kind of normality. When I arrived I told the site agent and general foreman I wouldn't be at work the following Wednesday because of the funeral. That event when it came round was every bit as distressing as I'd expected it to be. There were somewhere between twenty and thirty people present. I honestly can't remember if hymns were sung. Who wants to sing at a time like that? I doubt if I could have kept my voice steady if I'd tried. I just recall standing or kneeling with my head bowed and my body rigid with grief. Mum was buried in the shade of a large oak tree. The headstone I'd ordered would bear the simple inscription 'Rose May Elizabeth Sharp, devoted wife and mother'. And that's exactly what she was.

I returned to work again the following day, a Thursday. To every working man pay day is the most important time of the week, always was always will be, and at Walden's our pay packets were handed out during the afternoon tea break. The

mess room as on most building sites was just a temporary
building, a wooden shed with insulation board tacked to the
inside and furnished with half a dozen wooden trestle tables.
Generally all the apprentices would sit together. At three
o'clock we all trooped in, the tea was poured and the
foreman arrived with the winnings. When he got to our table
however there was no packet for me. Instead the foreman
handed me a letter from the bottom of his tray. 'You've
earned so much this week, Sharp, they couldn't get it all in
the packet,' he said. I opened the envelope and took out a
letter. It read as follows: 'Dear Sharp, It has come to my
notice that you have taken time away from work without
written consent. Therefore your wages have been suspended
until such time you give a written explanation for your
absence.' It was signed L. Walden, Managing Director, the
man who had not looked at me the day he employed me.
From the site agent down everyone knew why I had not
been at work. I had buried my mum only yesterday and now
to get such a cruel letter felt like the deepest cut of all. I went
straight over to the office and told them in my best 'industrial
language' what I thought of the letter. The following
Monday I was given my wages, but after that letter I had
decided that as soon as I finished my apprenticeship in a few
months' time I would be off.

That October my indentured period came to an end, but
in the event I decided to see the winter out. I booked my
holidays in early. As soon as I had my week's pay plus two
weeks' holiday money in my hand I spoke to the site agent

and asked very meekly, 'Does the firm still employ me while I'm on holiday?' 'Of course they do, you idiot!' he laughed. 'They pay your National Insurance, don't they?' 'Good,' I said. 'In that case you can take my two weeks' holiday as notice: I'm off.' And that was that. From that day on I never wanted to be on PAYE again and have remained self-employed ever since.

9

'Dad, do you mind if I ask you something?'

'Hmm?'

We were sat down at the kitchen table in Spring Terrace having just finished our evening meal. Dad had the newspaper open in front of him and was reading an item about plans for a channel tunnel. People in the building industry had already been speculating about the money they might be able to earn if the project went ahead. As someone who liked working in the fresh air I didn't fancy the idea of being stuck underground in a two and four gang for hours on end, however high the wages. Besides, if this tunnel ever got off the ground, so to speak, they may not require the use of traditional bricklayers, unlike the original London Underground, which was built largely by Irish immigrant workers. Anyway, I'd been speculating about something else, something closer to home and it had been on my mind ever

95

since my mum had passed away, which was now almost a
year ago. It's strange how when someone very close dies
everything else goes on just the same, and yet inside you feel
the whole world has changed, which for you it has. With the
logical awareness that the person has gone there remains the
unbearable familiarity of their presence. I could still hear my
mum's voice around the house and see her face across the
table, or imagine any minute she would walk into the room
and lay a loving hand on my shoulder as she passed by in the
midst of one of her many chores. This closeness is both
comforting and intensely painful. The one you loved is with
you yet of course not with you. My dad, I could tell, still felt
her presence and the loss very keenly. The shock caused by
her swift, violent departure was for both of us hidden in the
cloak of routine. He was still getting up early each morning
and cycling off to Cope and Cope, spending his days
expertly shaping and hammering metal. In the evening he'd
mount his bike and pedal home again. The only difference
now on his return journeys was that he'd no longer stop off
to pick flowers for my mum. Apart from the absence of
flowers, though, everything else in the house was physically
unaltered. The black iron grate stood solid and timeless,
though polished less frequently now. The bevelled mirror
hung in the same position, and the kitchen table remained
unmoved, its sturdy turned wooden legs bearing the same
small patterns in the grain I knew so intimately, an
unchanged part of the minute geography of my childhood.
I looked up at the mirror now and remembered my mum's

face reflected there the night they had broken the news and handed me my birth certificate. I felt again the tight embrace of her arms and her flowing tears on my face, the awful, uncontrollable twisting of her features with emotion. 'Please don't turn against us, David, please …' The mirror had seen all. What had it witnessed the day I first arrived at Spring Terrace, I wondered? If the mirror could speak I'd willingly have asked it. When Mum was there I'd never have dreamed of distressing her, but Dad was the one who'd first broached the subject of my origins, and right now was the only one who could tell me more about the matter.

'What son?' he replied without looking up from the paper.

'Where did you get me from?'

I noticed him stiffen, his fingers holding the page in mid turn for a moment before replying 'It's not important, it's water under the bridge.' 'That's not good enough,' I said immediately. 'You said I had a right to know before, well, I'd like to know a bit more now.'

My dad shot me a quick look and said, 'If you must know we got you out of a paper.' 'A paper, what paper?' 'The *Reading Mercury*, now pour me another cup of tea, would you.'

Reading Concert Hall is a lovely old building which in 1964 still housed the Reading Library. Apart from being a place to borrow books, your local library was in those days the first port of call for information. The librarians, usually schoolmistress types with a list of dos and don'ts about what was permitted on the premises and quick to shush anyone who talked above a whisper, would, if they couldn't answer your enquiry themselves, look it up or point you in the right direction. Based on my dad's information I had already narrowed my field of enquiry, and was looking for back numbers of the *Reading Mercury* for the year 1942, the year of my birth, and one week after his short reply to my question at the tea table I made my way to the library to conduct my research.

'I don't know that you'll find every issue for those months here,' said the lady librarian as she offloaded two large cardboard boxes into my arms.

'Thank you,' I said, 'that's very helpful.' At least I hoped it would be. My dad had definitely said the *Mercury*, though he couldn't recall the exact date that he and Mum had seen the advert. I opened the first box and began working my way through the classifieds at the back of each paper. This was interesting in itself, and it was remarkable to see how many servants were still employed in the 1940s, with loads of demand for gardeners especially. There was a shortage of 'help' obviously due to the war, and many of the ads specified that the applicants be over military age. So if you weren't young enough to earn a crust risking life and limb on the battlefields of Europe you could always pull up spuds for the gentry back home, and get a tithe cottage thrown in, providing your wife agreed to 'assist in the house occasionally'. After about an hour leafing through the editions I came across the following under the heading of 'Personal'. It read:

> WANTED: HOME FOR BABY BOY,
> AGE 1 MONTH; COMPLETE SURRENDER.
> WRITE BOX 173, MERCURY, READING.

My stomach gave a little flip. The date and the wording seemed to fit the bill, but how could I be sure it referred to me? It was the first advertisement of its kind I had come across. I went through a few more of the subsequent issues of the paper but there was nothing even mentioning children in the classifieds. It had to be me, but it seemed incredible. Above the entry was one from a band who needed musical instruments and below was a second-hand furniture dealer's advertisement. I suppose my ad was also 'house clearance' in a way! I read it again and again but still couldn't believe it. The fact it was just a box number was frustrating, but understandable. I suppose I could hardly have hoped for a name and address. I wondered if advertising unwanted children was legal in the 1940s. Apparently so or otherwise the *Mercury* surely wouldn't have printed it. Though perhaps being a time of war blind eyes had been turned. I took the paper up to the desk and asked the librarian for two copies. 'Find what you were looking for?' she smiled. 'Yes, thanks,' I said, though the truth was 'Yes and no.' The ad, though crucial, was only the first piece of a puzzle, and finding it had only made me realise how important the other pieces were, and how hard they might prove to track down. Who had given me away and why? Were they still alive? Did I have other relatives, brothers, sisters, what were they like? My imagination was already working overtime. I hadn't told Dad about my visit to the library. I didn't want to upset him or give him the impression I was ungrateful or dissatisfied with the life he and Mum had provided for me. Now having found the advert, I would continue to conduct my enquiry in secret.

10

When I was a kid we'd never gone away as a family on holiday. That wasn't so unusual for those days I suppose. But looking back I think this may have had something to do with my mum. She never seemed to venture far from our front door. Even when I was older and had a car, if I suggested a shopping trip to Reading or Henley-on-Thames, she would get very anxious. Much later on I put two and two together and realised she was probably agoraphobic. However this didn't keep me confined and from around the age of ten or eleven I had plenty of opportunities to go away since I was a member of Baden-Powell's great institution, the Boy Scouts, and when the school holidays came round I would be merrily off to camp with our local troop, the 75 Reading Free Church Scouts. We would catch the bus to Caversham where we'd load our kitbags onto wooden hand carts with large wheels, a bit like old gun carriages, and from there make our way on foot to camp.

The main campsite for scouts in our area was situated a little way outside Reading, a place known as Milestone Woods. Milestone was an enchanting location of seemingly endless mature trees, beech, oak and elm, a wonderful place for boys to pitch their tents and explore, waking under canvas to the low warble of a wood pigeon and the soft shuffling of leaves in the breeze. Far from the clocks and bells of school we would spend the days picking our way through the bracken, with the sunlight dappling the ground and birdsong always somewhere high above us. The woods were our private kingdom, a glorious open space for us to tramp and climb around, looking and listening and idling away the time the way kids do, with not a care in the world, little savages at one with nature and lost in the rich, rugged splendour of it all. The things I learnt there remain with me to this day – cooking on an open fire, recognising the various types of trees from their leaves and shape, which berries and mushrooms are edible and which poisonous, the differing prints and droppings of fox and ferret.

Today Milestone Woods would undoubtedly be a nature reserve, either coming under the official green belt or zealously guarded by the Campaign for the Protection of Rural England. The reason I say this is because some time after those carefree youthful days under canvas beneath the canopy of the great trees, I was to return to Milestone Woods. It must have been a decade later in fact and needless to say I was no longer wearing a woggle. It wasn't only me who had changed; my old campsite had too. As I looked around trying to piece together my memories of the place it was actually impossible since almost every tree had been felled, every bush bulldozed out of existence. Milestone Woods was no longer a woods; it had been wiped from the face of the earth. Welcome to Caversham Park Village.

This was now the early 1960s, and people my age, baby boomers by then in their twenties, were looking to become homesteaders, to buy a house of their own and start a family. Milestone Woods, many of whose trees had stood perhaps for a hundred or more years, was about to plant the next generation. The whole area was now one massive building site, with men and machinery crawling all over the churned-up earth. Donkey-jacketed surveyors were squinting through theodolites and waving their arms, JCBs rumbled and scraped, scouring out foundation channels, and pallet-loads of breezeblocks were being lowered to the ground from the backs of lorries. Here and there the first courses of brickwork were already rising, the walls of the new homes taking shape.

And that day returning to the site of the old Milestone Woods I was to become part of it all for the next eighteen months. Now a couple of years out of my apprenticeship and a fully fledged 'trowel', I was among the various small firms of subcontractors or 'subbies' as they were known, who together would raise Caversham Park Village. I was part of a 'five and two split' gang, meaning that there were five bricklayers and two hod carriers. We were on price work, in other words, paid according to the amount we did, with all the money we earned split equally between us at the end of the week. Although the hod carriers were on the same money as the bricklayers I didn't begrudge them a penny. The harder we brickies worked the faster they had to go to keep up with us. Usually the hoddies would start half an hour earlier in the morning so that when we arrived the scaffolding was loaded with bricks and mortar, and more often than not they'd stay on after the brickies had gone home to load out more bricks in front of us. Being all price work, the more we grafted the more money we took home at the end of the week. There didn't seem to be much, if any, 'quality control' over the work, and I don't recall anyone coming round to check what we were doing. The houses were of a uniform design, mostly three-bedroom link-detached with garages in between, so once you'd done one or two you knew the heights and distances of the brickwork and it was just a matter of repetition. There were to be around 1500 units in all and I think the finished houses sold for between four and five thousand pounds.

Working conditions were pretty basic and today's health and safety people would have a fit if they went back. For a start no one wore hard hats, which are usually insisted on nowadays. In the site hut was a gas ring and frying pan where those who wanted to could knock up bacon and eggs, making sure the overnight footprints of the rats in the lard were well melted away first. Most people brought sandwiches in. We would knock off for ten minutes for a cup of tea at about ten in the morning and maybe for fifteen to twenty minutes from about 1pm. Food breaks were kept to an absolute minimum. If we weren't laying bricks we weren't earning. I generally kept a bar of chocolate in my pocket to eat during the afternoon, but one particular day I'd forgotten to bring one. We were doing top-outs at the time (building gables and chimneys) and as we worked on I became hungrier by the minute. It wasn't helped by a gorgeous smell of roast pork wafting past me. I didn't know of a restaurant anywhere nearby but this wonderful smell just engulfed me – oh, what I wouldn't give for just a small plate of that! When the hod carrier brought the next load of mortar I asked him where the restaurant was. 'Restaurant?' he said. 'Oh, that's the crematorium chimney you can smell. They always put a batch through about this time of day.' I looked across to where he was pointing and sure enough the Allhallows Road Crematorium was sending up smoke signals that someone's dearly departed was returning to their maker. My hunger disappeared instantly, replaced by sickness and revulsion at what I had been thinking moments earlier. To this day, although the aroma has gone the memory lingers on and pork is still very much my least favourite meat.

Most of the time on site it was go, go, go, heads down and arses up, house a day, street a week stuff, day in day out. If it rained you got wet; in fact whatever the weather you just kept going. In the winter, when the sun went down we'd burn the empty cement bags to provide enough light to carry on working. It was certainly a young man's life, with most of the guys like me being in their twenties. You didn't get the work through the Labour Exchange but via word of mouth, meeting in pubs and passing on information among a circle of tradesmen – networking I suppose you'd call it. Everyone on the site was on 'the lump' – which meant we were paid in cash with no deductions for tax or National Insurance. All you had to do was sign a receipt book, though not necessarily with your own name. I must admit on a couple of occasions I signed as Mr D. Duck, or was it Mr M. Mouse? Time does funny things to your memory. Pinocchio would have been more appropriate really I suppose.

Come Thursday the leaders of the various gangs booked in all the work that had been done during that week to the main subcontractor, who would come round the following day with the money. In his younger days this contractor had been a professional boxer. I think his name was Shiel and his claim to fame was having had a couple of fights against a big name in boxing at that time, Johnny Prescott. Come each Friday at lunchtime out at Caversham Park you had the opportunity to double your money. All you had to do was challenge this guy to a bare-knuckle contest right there on the site. If you drew blood from him he would double your wages. The other side of the coin, however, was that if he drew blood from you, you received bugger all for your whole week's graft. At that time a brickie on PAYE earned about twenty quid a week, with those on the lump on forty to forty-five pounds and the chance to double it to eighty or ninety was tempting, if you fancied your chances. The temptation proved too much for some of my co-workers, their thinking being if they could handle themselves when things kicked off down the pub on a Friday night they could certainly look after themselves against an old man in his forties. But I never saw that 'old man' beaten. We would all gather round as he ducked and dived for a few minutes as the latest contender swung out. The 'reigning champ' would eventually get bored and slap him, usually on the nose, drawing some rich claret and richer curses from his opponent.

'See you Mick – see you Jim – if you can't be good be careful!' With our wallets full of cash and spirits high with demob fever, Fridays were always eagerly awaited. Some of the guys headed straight for the nearest pub to commence one long piss-up which would last the whole weekend, after which they'd arrive back on site the following Monday, penniless, to start grafting all over again. 'Pissing it all up against a wall' was a commonly used expression for how some building workers invested their earnings. And in those days many people, office workers and tradesmen alike would take their cars to the pub, either spending the whole evening there before driving home or going on a crawl of the hostelries on route and ending up in their local. There was then no official limit on the amount of alcohol a person could drink before getting behind the wheel of a car, and the breathalyser was as yet unheard of. Drink-driving was therefore common and even considered a bit of a laugh by some. Seatbelts were not compulsory either (it wasn't till some years later that even their voluntary use was recommended, with Jimmy Saville urging us to 'clunk click every trip') so those who drank and drove could endanger their own safety as much as that of other road users. At that time Julie and I were saving up for a deposit on a house, so although I liked a drink most of my wages went into the building society.

However there was another way you could spend your money before you even left work. Most Friday afternoons a large Ford Zephyr would roll up on site, towing behind it a tatty old caravan. The Zephyr would draw the caravan to some discreet position and park up. Now there were two doors in this caravan, one at the front and one on the opposite side at the back. Inside (so I was told) was a sliding partition. I suppose it was a bit like a Mr Whippy van without the chimes, though it wasn't ice cream that was on sale. One Friday afternoon in winter we'd been working till gone dusk. I'd cleaned off my tools and packed away and was just heading for my Ford Anglia estate to drive home when I heard a woman's voice. 'Davy, is that you?' it said. I looked across to the caravan. Only one person had ever called me Davy – Pat of Cope and Cope and Greenham Common fame! I made my way over towards the caravan. 'I thought it was you,' said the woman's voice again. 'How is my little Davy?' It was Pat all right. I hadn't seen her since my rapid departure from Cope and Cope some seven years ago. Now here she was stood in the doorway of this old caravan, with a dim light glowing behind her. 'You're not so little any more,' she said, looking me up and down, and sounding a bit like Diana Dors in some cheap film melodrama. In seven years she had aged considerably. Her frizzy bottle-blonde hair was pulled back in a bun and she had a scar about three-inches long on her cheek. A fag hung from the corner of her mouth. I peered at her through the gloom, framed in this eerie light. I wondered if there was anyone else in the caravan. 'How are you doing, Pat?' I said. 'Don't you work at Cope and Cope anymore?' She took the cigarette from her mouth. 'No, me and my mate do this full time now. Some transformers went missing and they accused me. Why would I want to nick fucking transformers? I wasn't going to take that lying down so I told them to stuff their job.' Bearing in mind her current occupation, 'taking things lying down' seemed a funny way to put it, but the irony was lost on her. We both looked up as someone approached the caravan. 'You'd better go – it looks like I've got a customer,' she said. 'Take care of yourself, Pat,' I replied. 'And you, Davy.' A shadowy male figure climbed the steps of the caravan and Pat disappeared inside. I was never to see her again. Throughout her career I imagine Pat had more partners than John Lewis. Over the years I have often wondered how her life panned out, and what became of her.

11

The question of the newspaper advert was still playing on my mind. The day I had found it in the library I had gone straight along to the offices of the *Reading Mercury*. 'Can you tell me who placed this advertisement please?' I asked. 'How interesting,' said the lady behind the desk as she scrutinised the photocopy. 'I wonder where that baby is now, poor thing – 1942! He must be how old now, um …?' 'Twenty-two,' I said, before she started taking her shoes off to do the arithmetic. 'Yes, that's right. Well, thank you for bringing this in to show us. We do sometimes display old editions of the paper in the window, show how times have changed.' 'Well, actually,' I said, 'I wanted to ask for some information. I'd like to know who placed the ad.' 'I'm afraid we don't disclose the details of advertisers unless they specify. That's why they have a box number you see, for confidentiality.' 'Well this was a long time ago,' I said. 'I'm afraid it doesn't make any difference, and in fact I don't think our records even go back as far as 1942. May I ask why you need to know?' 'I'm the baby boy.' At this she looked at me with the same curious look she'd given the photocopy. Now I was the historical artefact. Maybe she was thinking how I'd look displayed in the window. 'My goodness me, I see,' she said as the information sank in. 'Well, I wish I could help but my hands are tied. You could always try a solicitor or private enquiry agent. Sorry.' 'Yes, thank you,' I said. 'Perhaps I'll do that.' As I left the *Mercury* office she said, 'I do hope it all works out.' What it was I wanted to 'work out' I wasn't at all sure. At that point I simply wanted to know who'd given birth to me and why I'd been dumped, in such a cut-and-dried fashion. If my search was successful there might follow consequences and complications, and not necessarily pleasant ones, but I would cross that bridge when I came to it.

The past could be sorted out all in good time. Right now it was my future that demanded attention, or rather our future, since Julie and I had now decided on a date for our wedding, and on the 18 September 1965 we were married at Bledlow Ridge Church near High Wycombe. It was a wonderful occasion. I know people usually say that about their wedding day, but it's with good reason; it is probably the one time in your life where all your friends and family gather together with the express intention of making you, and your partner, feel special, and of course, to have a good time themselves in the process. (No wonder Elizabeth Taylor and

Richard Burton got married to each other twice.) Naturally there was a tinge of sadness, felt by both my dad and me, that Mum wasn't there to see the pair of us walk down the aisle that sun-kissed autumn day. She'd have been so proud, I know. When I carried Julie over the threshold, our house in Didcot became a home. Married life had begun.

Working on Caversham Park Village gave me a better grasp of how the building game operated. The main building contractor, whose suited and booted executives and site agents put up the flags and polished up the show home, engaged subcontractors, who in turn hired and paid the small gangs of tradesmen like us. In the process the subcontractors took their cut. Fair dos, these intermediaries provided a service, but I could now see there was no mystique about it, and that there was no law stating you had to go through them to get work. What had dawned on me I suppose was that you could cut out the middle man, and all things being equal, be better off for it. After eighteen months at Caversham Park I felt like a change of scene, and with more confidence in my ability to approach the head honchos directly and negotiate, I decided to form my own gang and get some work direct from a main contractor. So with a four and two gang (four bricklayers and two hod carriers) I got the start on a site to the west of Reading called Purley Beeches, wedged between the main railway line and the A329.

The builder at Purley Beeches was a local firm called West New Homes that was turning out an estate of houses similar to Caversham Park. At this point though the building industry was going through a bit of a slump and my prices reflected the fact. Without question my rates were absolute crap, but current market forces dictated that even in a good week I could pick up little more than sixty to seventy pounds. I must admit things were hard going, especially as I was now paying a mortgage, Julie and I having bought our own brand new three-bed semi with integral garage for just over three thousand pounds. Admittedly we'd put down a deposit of a thousand pounds, so a third of the property was already ours so to speak, but the deeds remained with the building society and the monthly payments went out come rain or shine.

Still, Purley Beeches wasn't a bad set-up. We had a decent crowd of men on the job and at least I was working. Things could only get better. At least that's what I thought till I arrived at work one morning to find several policemen guarding the entrance to the site. Parked up outside were some of my colleagues. 'What's going on Alan?' I asked one of the other brickies. 'Someone dug up a body?' 'Not quite,' said Alan, 'they've only gone tits-up, haven't they.' 'Who has?' 'West New Homes – they're brassic mate, gone bust.' Bankruptcy, foreclosure, whatever you like to call it, had descended, and it seemed that overnight West New Homes had gone well and truly west. I said, 'So does that mean we're all down the road or what?' 'Looks that way mate, we're just waiting to get in and pick up our tools.' At this point one of the plasterers came over. 'They're saying everything's got to stay put.' 'What about our gear?' said Alan. 'Property of the official receiver – mixers, dumpers, you name it, they want it, even the fucking Brooke Bond tea.' 'But I've got tools in the shed,' I said. 'They're my property.' 'They're not letting anyone in.' 'They can't do that!' 'They have.' 'What are we going to do then?' said Alan. Several of the other lads had turned up now. Many of them, like me, had tools and equipment stored on site. The plumbers in particular were very concerned since they had a lot of materials in situ and copper piping doesn't come cheap. After a discreet powwow we hatched a plan. I went over and chatted to the old bill by the fence, asking what was going on, just to keep them talking. Meanwhile a few of the lads snuck round the back of the site and broke open the sheds. Ten minutes later they returned with a van-load of our tools and other gear which was then distributed to its rightful owners. Take away a tradesman's tools and you might as well cut off his hands. The official receiver could whistle, he wasn't having my trowel. Years later I heard that when Rod Hull got into financial difficulties he was allowed to keep Emu since he was classed as the tools of his trade, without which he couldn't hope to settle his debts. Then he went and fell off his roof adjusting the TV aerial, poor bloke. Anyway, in this case, we tradesmen weren't even the ones who'd gone bankrupt, but they'd attempted to seize our property nonetheless. First to pick at the carcass of West New Homes would no doubt be the Inland Revenue, followed by the big boys, suppliers of materials, architects and what have you. We tradesmen were at the bottom of the heap as far as creditors were concerned. The insolvency lawyers were no doubt already rubbing their hands together. Later that day I paid the rest of the gang the wages I owed them and went home.

That afternoon I phoned round to try to find some alternative work. This proved difficult. The slump was obviously worse than I had realised. The next day I sat down over a cup of tea and contemplated my next move. Though my wages had stopped coming in those mortgage payments were still going out along with all the other bills, and being out of work was the last thing I needed. My thoughts were interrupted by the phone ringing. 'Could I speak to David Sharp?' said the man on the other end. 'Speaking' I replied. 'Oh, I'm glad I caught you,' he went on. 'My name is Alan Reason. I'm the managing director of Reason Homes. I've been brought in by United Dominion Trust …' 'Who are they?' I said 'They're the loan company that have sent West New Homes into receivership. Basically United Dominion have asked me to get Purley Beeches moving again and I wonder if you would be interested in coming back to work for my company?' This sounded promising. Mr Reason then said, 'I've been looking at the books and going through your prices – however did you make a living wage? I mean your rates are three or four years out of date.' I didn't say anything, but if you had looked into my eyes at that moment all you'd have seen was five-pound notes, lots of them. 'Would you be prepared to come down to the site for a chat? Shall we say 9am tomorrow?' I readily agreed and told Julie the good news.

So next morning there I was back at Purley Beeches, at present still devoid of activity. I saw a middle-aged guy in a suit and gumboots running his eye over the semi-formed houses. On seeing me he came over and shook my hand energetically. 'Morning Mr Reason,' I said. 'Oh please, call me Alan. May I call you David?' 'Yes,' I said. Mr Reason – Alan – immediately took out a sheaf of papers and with a red pencil went down a list of my quotes. Striking through the 'out of date prices' he wrote a new amount alongside each one underlining it and showing me as he did so. Every one of my 'crap' prices was raised, in some cases doubled. What a turn-up. That night I phoned around the guys and invited them back on board. None of them had been able to find work yet and so we were all delighted to get the start again so quickly and with a pay rise to boot.

Our gang was the first back on site at Purley Beeches. Next day the carpenters turned up, and one by one the other tradesmen followed suit. After a week or so it was a fully working site again and I was earning better than before. Everything was going well until one Thursday afternoon, when as usual the quantity surveyor brought our pay round, while at the same time booking in the work we had completed that week. As the QS handed me my cheque he said, 'Dave we want you and all your men off site now, you're finished.' I looked at him a bit gob-smacked. 'Why, is there a problem with our work?' 'No, no, that's all fine. It's just the way Mr Reason works.' 'Meaning?' I said. 'Well, between you and me Dave, and I know this is going to sound a bit underhand, but when he starts a job he tempts one subbie back with more money so the others will follow. You were the only one to get paid better rates. In fact, because there's not much work about all the others are on less money than they were before. Sorry Dave.' So, Mr (call me Alan) Reason had dangled a hook in front of me, a hook baited for one of the seven deadly sins – GREED. And I had swallowed that hook, the line and sinker too. I had led the other trades back on site like some kind of sacrificial lamb to the slaughter. Alan Reason had told the other blokes that Dave Sharp was happily back at Purley Reaches so they'd think it was a good number, forgetting to mention he was paying me over the odds, and forgetting to tell me that I'd only be there for a few weeks. It was a confidence trick. That day I realised a very important truth; if it sounds too good to be true it probably is. The upshot was that I had to go back and lay off the gang for a second time and lose a lot of street cred in the process. Ever felt skewered? And do you know, I am still owed the price of building three of the houses on that site from when West's went bust. It was just for the brickwork shells admittedly but still a good bit of money. I think about it whenever I pass the Purley Beeches estate. I wonder how many times those houses have changed hands since then, and how many other tradesmen 'call me Alan' manipulated. As they say, you live and learn.

12

1966 was a good year for me, with England winning the World Cup and the birth of our daughter Marion (not necessarily in that order of importance). We had only been married three months when Julie announced that she was pregnant. New house, new baby syndrome I suppose. I've often thought if childless couples moved to a new house instead of embarking on a costly course of fertility treatment they would save a great deal of money. Marion was born in St George's Hospital in Wallingford, which is now a housing estate. At that time, St George's was ruled with a rod of iron by 'Matron'. It was said even the doctors treated Matron with kid gloves and though barely five feet tall, her authoritative reputation was such that no one argued with her. I dare say there were a few jokes among the medical staff about St George's own resident 'dragon', but she clearly knew her job and did it diligently.

A woman's experience of giving birth today is starkly different to what it was in the 1960s. In those far-off days the mother and baby would spend a week in hospital and that was for a routine birth. By contrast, when Marion gave birth to our grandsons she spent just twenty-four hours in hospital, barely time for a cup of tea. And of course fathers were not present during the birth as they are encouraged to be nowadays, as well as going along to all the antenatal classes. The first thing that struck you on entering St George's in the 1960s was the strong odour of carbolic; everything seemed to smell of it. And 'woe betide' any cleaner who didn't do their job properly, for Matron would soon be on their case. In those days you went into hospital expecting to be treated for whatever illness or accident had struck you down in the first place. If you did leave in a wooden box, it wasn't from having picked up some superbug waiting to pounce on you as soon as you were wheeled into the ward. The high standards of the traditional matrons as regards house-keeping must surely have played a big part in keeping hospitals relatively germ-free then.

It was a glorious mid September day when I was finally told I could pick up Julie and our new daughter from the hospital. All the babies born at the hospital were the responsibility of the Matron until it was their time to go home; she would not allow any of the parents to carry their newborn out of the ward and we were no exception. On arrival at the main door of St George's Matron finally handed over our daughter to Julie. As she did so she touched my arm whilst looking at Julie, and said in a voice I can only describe as being as soft as an angel's fart, 'Remember my dear, he is still your biggest baby.' I was really touched by that. Then she turned to me. In an instant her sunny demeanour had turned to the bitter frost of winter, as with a glaring eye she rasped, 'Remember, six weeks – don't be an animal!' Apparently every couple received this same no-nonsense advice when they left the hospital with the new addition to their families. The St George's Matron continued to reside locally after her retirement and maintained a life-long interest in the infants who'd been in her charge. She knew 'her babies' even when they towered above her and had babies of their own.

After our sudden lay-off from Reason Homes it hadn't been too long before the lads and I were back in work and my financial worries eased. Being self employed we obviously had no holiday or sick pay, and whenever possible I'd keep a bit in the bin to cover these eventualities. Fortunately my health was pretty good. Inflation was a big issue in those days (as I write this, many predict it's coming back with a vengeance again) with rising prices causing higher pay demands that in turn fuelled the cost of living and so the spiral continued. Alan Reason hadn't been talking complete bull about my rates being out of date, for soon afterwards they actually were. To get what he wanted he had just exaggerated the fact that at that time everyone expected to charge more year on year, or even month on month for the supply of their labour and skills. People were now talking about something called 'runaway inflation' and Harold Wilson's new Labour government was proposing a pay freeze. The unions didn't like it one bit. The building industry wasn't heavily unionised and that's the way the big contractors liked it. We self-employed tradesmen were free, if that's the right word, to set our own wages, though whether anyone would pay them was of course another matter.

Now that Julie and I were settled in our home and into a routine I began to think again about what the lady in the *Reading Mercury* office had suggested. I did still want to trace the source of that advert, and I therefore decided to check out the solicitors. 'Very interesting, very interesting indeed,' said one of the partners at the first firm I called on. 'So you think you can find out who placed the ad?' I said. 'Oh very possibly, very possibly, we can certainly begin straight away.' I asked how much it would cost. 'Well, that depends of course.' 'On what?' 'How long it takes.' 'Well, can you give me a rough estimate of your fees?' 'Two hundred and fifty pounds.' 'Crikey, as much as that!' I said. That was three weeks' wages. 'These things are costly I'm afraid.' 'Well, if you can definitely come up with the goods.' 'We can do our very best. We would of course require payment in advance. And then if things do take a little longer any additional costs can be spread over a period.' Additional costs. So the two-and-a-half-hundred was just to get the ball rolling. They could spin the case out for as long as they liked and were offering no guarantee of success. It'd be giving them a blank cheque and perhaps getting nothing for it. Other firms I went to told more or less the same story; yeah, love to help, show us the money, we'll let you know if we find anything. Even if I could have afforded the arm and a leg the bandits were asking it would have been pointless without some evidence of what justified the fees. Maybe there was a simple way I could do the tracing myself, and I couldn't help wondering if it was simply my ignorance these professionals were attempting to trade on.

Perhaps there was a deeper reason the door to the past remained shut to me. In 1966 we'd all learned the terrible facts about the Moors murders: Myra Hyndley and Ian Brady had been jailed for life for torturing and killing two children and a teenage boy. The details of what this pair had done were so horrific it had normally calm and collected individuals in tears, howling for the rope, or both. The mother of one of the victims was to publicly declare that if either of the murderers were ever released, she would personally avenge her child's death by way of an eye for an eye. Few doubted her sincerity. The fact that such sadistic monsters had been walking around would surely make anyone reflect thankfully on the basic human goodness of their parents and guardians, friends, family and neighbours. After all it could have been anyone who'd landed in the clutches of Hyndley and Brady, and though this might sound superstitious or extreme, I did wonder not for the first time if someone or something – God or destiny – had steered me into the loving bosom of Mr and Mrs Sharp of 1, Spring Terrace. Who knows, for me to stir up the past by questioning the rhyme and reason behind my happy fate, might even be to tempt it.

Before we knew it our baby daughter Marion was a baby no more, and was soon toddling, walking and talking. As well as being curious about her world, exploring the intricate shapes and colours of every flower, blade of grass and new toy, she was as keen as any young child to express herself, sometimes very forcibly. In that she was certainly in keeping with the spirit of the age. Everywhere you looked some John, Paul, George or Ringo was expressing himself – not always as charmingly as our little girl. Along with the Stones and the Beatles came all the rest of the pop music and fashion razzamatazz. Not every part of the country slavishly followed London and Liverpool of course. Tim Rice once said that the swinging sixties consisted of three people at a party and everyone else trying to find out where it was. I don't think it was Didcot or Wallingford. I do remember mini-skirts being worn by the young – and often not-so-young ladies of our neighbourhood. The latter in particular would often prompt disapproving remarks from the prudish: 'Look at that – mutton dressed as lamb!' frumpy onlookers would comment from their garden gates as some woman of allegedly inappropriate size or age would shimmy by dressed in the style of Lulu or Helen Shapiro. One thing was for sure; someone in the rag trade had their head screwed on when they marketed the mini-skirt – just double your profits by halving the amount of fabric used.

The sixties' music of course got everywhere. There was always somebody or other on the building site with a scratchy transistor going from sun-up to sunset, though contrary to popular belief, listening to country and western didn't automatically mean you were a cowboy builder. Down the pub the jukebox would be belting out 'The Green, Green Grass of Home' or 'Penny Lane' till closing time. Listening to Alan Freeman's *Pick of the Pops* on the radio every Sunday night was a must for teenagers, while the older generation (nowadays they'd be called grumpy old men) tended to remain loyal to 'Sing Something Simple', featuring a traditional repertoire in which you could 'at least understand what they're singing about – not like all these long-haired young fellers nowadays!' The young fellers' hair got longer, and 'flower power' came in, preaching peace and love helped along by happy baccy. In London there were sit-ins and demonstrations, students getting stroppy with their teachers and taking over the colleges. All around the world, the tail seemed to want to wag the dog. And perhaps that was right, if the dog was a bad one. In particular, many viewed the US government and its activities in Vietnam as a very bad dog. Heavyweight boxing champion Cassius Clay changed his name to Muhammad Ali and refused the draft, unwilling to fight in an unjust war. Anyone seeing the newspaper colour supplements of that time, with their uncompromising pictures of the horrific effects of napalm and other weapons on human beings, would find it hard to disagree with the man who floated like a butterfly and stung like a bee. On 4 April 1968 another American, who'd taken a different kind of stand, Martin Luther King, was killed by an assassin's bullet. His words 'I have a dream' became famous. But he also said, 'I may not get there with you.' A dreamer, but one with no illusions about the kind of world he lived in.

As the sixties drew to a close people began to look back and assess how Britain and the world had changed in the preceding ten years. One landmark event in the middle of the decade had been the death of Winston Churchill. He had been given an elaborate state funeral, treated indeed as royalty, which for the wartime generation, to all intents and purposes he was. The funeral was televised and teachers up and down the land interrupted their lessons, wheeling TV sets in front of their somewhat uncomprehending pupils. To those who'd experienced the war, it would always be seen as Churchill's finest hour, and his place in their minds and hearts as the saviour of the nation was permanent. In many ways his death did signify the end of an era. Challenging the old class system which Churchill represented were characters on film and TV like Michael Caine's 'Alfie', a cockney artful dodger for our times, ducking and diving and cocking a snook at authority, while pulling the birds left, right and centre.

There did seem to be money about at that time, or at least, people were spending it. Traditionally there had tended to be the thrifty approach towards buying furniture, clothes, radiograms, washing machines, cars and the like, with hire purchase or the 'never-never' looked on with caution, even suspicion. This attitude was to change. Soon it would become the in thing to have credit cards. Up to then many men in my trade had never even had a bank account. And who would have thought that before long we'd be getting our cash out of vending machines in the wall, just like a packet of bubble gum or bar of chocolate? I remember seeing Reg Varney of *On the Buses* fame doing an advert for the first cashpoint machine. You kept expecting to hear him say 'Crikey, 'ere comes Blakey', followed by Blakey's drawl of 'I'll 'ave you Butler!' Whereas once upon a time you might save long and hard for a three-piece suite or a car, you could now do what the rich did – sign for it. It was all there for the taking. It was the start of the whole 'have it now, pay later' way of life.

If the school kids of 1965 had been bored by all the fuss about some fuddy-duddy old codger in the government having kicked the bucket, those youngsters watching TV in 1969 had something to get excited about. Men walking on the surface of the moon were worth any number of flag-draped coffins crawling down Whitehall to the dirge of a military band. When those first images of the astronauts were seen, it must have seemed to many children like their sci-fi comic books had come to life. 'Wow, that's more like it, Miss!' One small step for Buzz, one huge buzz for a whole generation.

Our own member of the very young generation, little Marion, was getting bigger, and of course, chattier. Old ladies in the street would gaze fondly at her and say to us wistfully, 'Oh, they grow up ever so quick you know; they really do …' The old ladies were right. Soon Marion would be starting school. Already she was asking lots of questions about anything and everything. I wondered, in a few years' time would I be sitting down with her and having a heart to heart about her family history? I reflected that it would be a shorter history than that of most families, stopping, or beginning if you like, rather abruptly at 1, Spring Terrace, supposedly in 1942. I could tell my daughter as much as I knew of course: the tearful revelation by my parents when I was aged fourteen; my later discovery of the complete surrender advert. But before I did that there was something else to consider. Marion had always known my dad as her granddad Percy. For his sake, and hers, I didn't want to cause any confusion and certainly no heartache. Those sleeping dogs couldn't be woken yet awhile. Of course that didn't stop me finding things out for myself, but how? If archaeologists could reconstruct ancient civilisations from fragments of pots and old bones then surely someone could help me track down two people who'd placed an ad in the local paper just a few years ago.

In November 1970 I obtained a full birth certificate from Somerset House in London. It gave my birth parents' names as Rose Lillian Violet Wort and Ernest Alfred Henry Wort. Ernest was a good old-fashioned name. I wondered if his mates called him 'Ernie'. Why had he given me up? And Rose, my birth mother, had the same name as my mum. This other Rose had been my mum once, I supposed. What had possessed her to advertise me in a newspaper? I had wondered at one point if I had in fact been only one month old when I arrived at Spring Terrace. I certainly had no memory of anywhere else. It was a lady called Kathleen who had confirmed this particular fact for me. As a little girl Kathleen had been evacuated from London during the Blitz and had lived with Mum and Dad at Spring Terrace. We had kept in touch and she had since revealed to me what she'd found one day on her return from Dunsden Primary School. 'I came into the cottage and there were nappies hanging round the grate. Auntie Rose was rocking this old second-hand pram and in it was a tiny little baby fast asleep. Auntie and Uncle, your mum and dad, just said you were called David, and that you would be staying for a while. I thought perhaps you'd been sent from London like me to get away from the bombs. You must have been only a few weeks' old. You did look sweet all tucked up and warm there by the fire. And Auntie and Uncle looked as pleased as punch.'

In the summer months, when I was working long hours on building sites into the light evenings I never thought much about the still unanswered question of my true parentage. The winter was another matter. When work was slack, with the weather not so conducive to my outdoor occupation, my mind often worked overtime. In the early 1970s, as a result of the strikes, came power cuts and blackouts, removing the distractions of TV and radio, and closing many pubs and other places of entertainment. The dark evenings hung heavily. Roll on summer we all thought.

Privately, however, I also reflected that with every year that passed, the probability of discovering and meeting my birth parents, and any other blood relatives I might have, grew smaller. Would I find out before it was too late, or would the author or authors of my complete surrender remain a mystery for eternity?

13

'Would you be prepared to write a letter, doctor?' I asked. 'Certainly, if you think it will help.' My dad's GP and I were discussing my dad. Dad had never quite got over the loss of my mum. I doubt if the idea of remarrying ever even crossed his mind. He had carried on with life placidly enough, but on his own it was never going to be the same, that was accepted and he wouldn't have it any other way. He remained at Cope and Cope as a sheet-metal worker till his retirement, having put in thirty years at the firm. This was the way it was then; people didn't chop and change employers and expected to have a job for life. This had all been fine for Dad and the familiarity and continuity had kept him going. The workplace was like another family. The problem was that since packing up work he was still living on his own at Spring Terrace. Again it was somewhere he'd known all his life and to uproot people from their surroundings at an advanced age is not always kind or wise, and with the memories of Mum in every nook and cranny of the place, who was I to tell him to leave? However, the old cottage was still as damp as it had been in my boyhood, and with Dad no longer in the prime of life his living conditions were now taking their toll. Rheumatism had already set in, and going out to the outside toilet in all weathers, not to mention lugging in coal for the fire, were now arduous tasks and risked further health problems. Julie and I saw him often enough and did what we could, but obviously we couldn't be there all the time. Dad needed a new home, with adequate heating and proper sanitation. The doctor's letter was to support our application to the council. We had also written to our local MP. If Bob Geldof could raise millions for worthy causes in Africa with Band Aid I didn't see why we couldn't succeed in a small campaign of our own here at home. After all, Dad had paid tax and National Insurance all his working life, and with all the new 'wealth creation' that Mrs Thatcher was now talking about it didn't seem unreasonable to ask that an honest, law-abiding citizen should have a decent roof over his head in his retirement. 'Thanks doctor,' I said, as he signed and gave me the letter detailing Dad's state of health and a recommendation for re-housing. 'Good luck,' he said, 'I hope it works out.'

It did. A few months later, courtesy of South Oxfordshire District Council my dad was installed in a brand new flat in a sheltered housing scheme in Woodcote. He'd been sad to leave Spring Terrace, that went without saying, but he adapted remarkably well to his new situation and quickly made friends in the local pub, the Red Lion, where he was soon regularly enjoying a pint or three of best bitter. One Saturday evening quite late, it must have been about 10.30pm because *Match of the Day* had started and Julie and I were watching TV when the phone rang. It was the warden from Dad's sheltered accommodation. 'Mr Sharp, I'm sorry to disturb you but it's about your father,' he said. 'What's wrong, is he ill?' I asked in alarm. 'Not ill exactly, he's drunk.' 'Oh, I'm sorry.' 'He's just thrown a Wellington boot at one of my ladies. You'll have to come and sort him out I'm afraid.' I explained the situation to Julie. 'Do you want me to come with you?' she said. 'Oh, no, no, I shan't be long,' I said picking up the spare key to Dad's flat. When I got there he was lying on his back on the bed spark out. Apart from one Wellington which for some mysterious reason he must have put back on again after undressing, he was stark naked. I also noticed that he'd omitted to take out his false teeth, and so to prevent the possibility of him choking I leaned over and gently removed them. He stirred a little as I did so and mumbled something. Rolling him over on his side I pulled the sheet and blanket up a bit to cover him and let myself out. I knew this wasn't the first time Dad had had too much ale and on the way home I resolved to do something about his drinking.

'Oh, hello Mr Sharp – I was expecting Mr Sharp senior!' It was Dad's GP, the same one who'd helped us get him moved. I had returned to his surgery to ask for his assistance again. 'Yes doctor, I made the appointment in my father's name because it's him I want to talk about.' 'Fire away.' 'It's his drinking.' 'What about it?' 'Well, he does drink rather a lot from time to time, and it's caused one or two problems.' I explained about the incident with the Wellington. The doctor smiled ruefully. 'Oh dear me I hope no one was hurt.' 'No, I don't think so,' I said. 'But I wonder if you'd mind having a word with him about his drinking, from a health point of view. He wouldn't listen to me, but coming from you he'd take it seriously.' The doctor nodded and looked thoughtful for a moment. 'I understand your concern,' he said at last, then continued slowly, 'The thing is Mr Sharp – how can I put this – there's only one thing certain about life, which is that one day it is going to end – for you, for me, for everyone. We're all going to die some day. Now your father, if you don't mind my saying so, is in the last years of his life, so why not let him enjoy himself? To tell you the truth, he and I often have a pint together!' When I arrived home Julie asked if I'd got it sorted out. I thought for a moment and then said, 'Yes, in a way I have. ' In fact it was me who had been sorted out.

On 4 June 1986 the phone rang. Julie took the call. It was the warden at dad's place again. 'Mrs Sharp, I'm sorry, your father-in-law has died.' We got over there straight away and saw that the police were just leaving. It had been a sudden death so the warden had had to notify them. Bracing myself I went in to his little flat. Dad was sitting in his favourite armchair. I approached him and stretched out my hand, then ran it gently over his full mop of silver hair. Later the post-mortem stated that a valve in his heart had just stopped working, and it seemed he hadn't suffered. There one minute, gone the next. I remember having very mixed emotions, a deep sadness but also selfish anger that he'd died when I still had so much to say to him. With my grief was an anguished sense of guilt and regret that those words could never be said now. I kept telling myself it had not been necessary, that he'd always known how much I cared. Dad was laid to rest alongside Mum in the Dunsden churchyard. It seemed looking back that he had 'enjoyed himself' in his twilight years, just as the doctor had ordered, and his passing had been smooth and relatively painless. Both he and my mum had given me everything possible. I couldn't have asked for more from them as parents. As Dad's coffin was lowered into the grave I thought back to Mum's tearful words all those years ago: 'Please don't turn against us David ...' How could I ever turn against two people who had wrapped me in nothing but the cocoon of their love for as long as I could remember? It was impossible.

With Dad gone however, the most important remaining link to my early life was severed. But was Dad the last link? Someone else must know something about what took place at 1, Spring Terrace around the November of 1942. With the puzzle no nearer completion and the trail receding ever further into the past, should I continue hoping that one day I would flush out the truth, or should I be the one to now concede defeat?

14

When I was a kid, the twenty-first century was an impossibly long way off, a time I could never believe myself actually living in. It was the world of Dan Dare and the *Eagle Annual*, where aliens routinely visited the earth and everyone whizzed around with jet packs on their backs. Well, here I was in the twenty-first century, and although space travel and supersonic flight had been around for some time, most people still got about as nature intended – in their cars! As far as we knew there'd been no sightings of visitors from other planets, though Patrick Moore with his *Sky at Night* programmes had kept alive our curiosity about what might be out there. His sense of wonder and enthusiasm for his subject has always been infectious. Contemplating the universe can be awe-inspiring. It's also sobering. Gazing out into the unknown vastnesses of space and an infinity of other worlds, thousands of light years away, how tiny and insignificant we suddenly seem, our teeming, tempestuous planet but a tiny speck among billions of other specks, floating in an eternal nothingness.

The Berlin Wall had come tumbling down long ago. What would my mum and dad have said about that? The fear of 'the bomb' was suddenly gone. (What would they have to worry about now – bird flu, global warming, terrorism?) Souvenirs of the Berlin Wall were quickly on sale, fragments of rubble and barbed wire stuck into little commemorative cases. I'm sure I could have made a good few bob at the time, if I'd scraped up some bits of brick from one of my jobs and put an advert on the internet. It was thought the internet had played some part in the further collapse of Communism, allowing people to talk and communicate freely. Knowledge is power they say, and with it the old Iron Curtain was dramatically drawn back. Behind it was not a cupboard full of monsters as many in the West had been led to believe, but ordinary people like us. When I was growing up, the countries of Eastern Europe had been dark, sinister places, a shadowy world of spies and assassins you only saw or heard about in films like *The Ipcress File*. Now people from the UK are buying holiday homes out there and Bulgaria's in the European Community, although, in Russia at least, the spies and assassins seem to be still about, and the Bear may yet growl again.

The millennium came and went and surprise, surprise, the world did not end in a bang or grind to a halt, despite all the talk about something called the 'Millennium Bug'. The main entertainment that year was provided by the Dome, though not for the reasons it was intended to. After Tony Blair's optimistic New Year's Eve bash there, the Dome became the nation's favourite white elephant, and endlessly pointed at as the reason we could have afforded better schools, hospitals, pensions and so on. Such things suddenly seemed trivial compared with what we all witnessed on 11 September 2001 when two hijacked aeroplanes were flown into the twin towers of the World Trade Center. Thousands of people trapped inside died as the vast structures collapsed and burned. That same evening Muhammad Ali came on television and told the world that Islam meant peace. America went to war. After Afghanistan and the Taliban there came, with Tony Blair's eager support, a massive strike against Saddam Hussein. The war in Iraq provoked fierce arguments in Parliament, as well as every pub and dinner table in the land. The arguments are still running, and will do so for a long time. Rest in peace the British soldiers and many innocent Iraqis who have been killed.

Since Dad's death, the words his doctor had spoken to me when I'd asked him to intervene over his drinking had echoed in my head. 'There's only one thing certain in this world; that some day, we're all going to die, you, me, everyone.' Everyone. The grim reaper was out there for me too, biding his time as surely as the farmer had waited patiently to harvest the cornfields of my childhood. 'At least I've got proper parents,' the little girl had said to me that day.

Well, so had I. And though both were now departed this life, they would always be my mum and dad. But there were also two people who'd produced me beforehand. That little girl had known more about me than I had, and used the knowledge to spite me. What else might she have known, what details? I could still, perhaps, find out more about Ernest and Rose Wort. Perhaps they were still alive, and there also might be other relatives out there somewhere.

'Let him enjoy himself,' the doctor had said of Dad. He had been right, and in a few years I would be the age my dad had been then. With a happy home life, fairly good health, an adequate income and regular football watching I couldn't deny I was enjoying life too, in my own way. But as they say in that old sketch about life being like a tin of sardines, there's always a little bit in the corner you can't get out. If the mystery surrounding my birth family had dwindled down to an insignificant bit of sardine during my busier working years, it was now becoming a bigger fish again. To use another image, one from the Bible, it was like the tiny grain of sand that, once it gets in your eye, feels like a brick. The cycle of life turns slowly, at some stages so slowly that its onward march is imperceptible to us. In youth we think we are immortal. What's that verse in which the poet observes that when as a child he sprawled and 'time crawled'? Then, on becoming a man 'time soon ran'. Eventually for the poet, time galloped. Time wasn't galloping for me, not yet at any rate.

Ever since we had been blessed with our lovely grandchild I'd been very excited to see him grow. It was sheer joy to see little Oliver laughing and smiling, as he took in and explored all the wonders of the world around him. And to soon hear him asking those endless questions about anything and everything. Babies communicate from day one of course, but like all families we were especially thrilled when he had begun to say his first words and we could chat with our new and much-loved young addition. Seeing Oliver develop, I felt even more strongly that I would like him to know about his family history. The writing I had started when he had been born was slowly taking shape. But curiously, as the structure of my story grew, the missing pieces about Oliver's ancestry on my side of the family seemed more and more like a gaping hole, making the rest in some ways meaningless. Like a chain, it seemed to be only as strong as its weakest link. In this case it was a completely missing link, the vital one that should, rightly, anchor our family history to the past. As I'd eventually done with Marion, I could tell Oliver all about the complete surrender advertisement of course, all that I myself knew. But it would be so much better if I could solve the puzzle and present him with the entire saga, whatever that turned out to be. On and off for the last few years, the search for my birth family had always been on the back burner, something to do 'tomorrow'. Now I was such a proud granddad the urge to resume the quest, get back on the trail, was keener than ever. I felt I owed it to myself and to my loved ones, especially Oliver. Tomorrow was here.

In February 2001 I placed an advertisement in the *Surrey Advertiser*. It read:

WORT – DO YOU KNOW, OR ARE
YOU RELATED TO ERNEST ALFRED HENRY
WORT AND ROSE LILLIAN VIOLET WORT
(NEE MOORE)?
IF SO, PLEASE WRITE TO BOX 4391.

Much to my disappointment the advert drew a blank, not a single reply. I had worded the entry to suggest that there might be an inheritance awaiting someone, but not even any potential fraudsters wrote back. In April we all celebrated Oliver's first birthday, and seeing his face light up when his cake appeared and everyone sang was sheer delight and just one of the many special moments we now had to treasure each day.

Summer came and went, and at the beginning of December Marion had a second child, another beautiful little boy. He was given the name Benjamin. Oliver now had a brother and companion, and we the most wonderful early Christmas present anyone could have asked for. Our lives and our happiness seemed complete. But though it might sound churlish, for me there was something missing. The jigsaw of the past had yet to be finished, for my own peace of mind and for the sake of the family. I had a duty to Oliver, and now to Benjamin too.

As was my custom at this time of year I telephoned Kathleen, the evacuee who'd stayed with my mum and dad at Spring Terrace during the war. We'd always kept in touch and I suppose since she'd always regarded my parents as an aunt and uncle, Kathleen was a sort of cousin to me. 'Happy Christmas Kathleen,' I said. 'How's Jim?' 'Oh, he's fine yes,' replied Kathleen. 'We're all very well here. The family are doing well I hope? – Lovely – How did you get on with your advert by the way, the *Surrey* ad?' 'No luck, not a single reply.' 'Oh, I am sorry.' 'Kathleen,' I said, 'I know I've asked you this before, but is there anything you can remember my parents saying about the people that gave me away?' 'No David, I can't recall any mention of that.' 'Do you remember anyone coming to Spring Terrace at all, before or after I turned up?' 'No, I'm sorry. I was only a child myself don't forget. The only people we saw were the neighbours, oh, and your Uncle Reg and his wife.' 'No one else?' 'David, I've told you all I know.' Kathleen's voice was insistent now. 'Yes, yes, of course, I'm sorry. Well, the only other option is solicitors. The trouble is they all want a fortune before they'll lift a finger, and then they don't guarantee results. They asked for two hundred and fifty quid before, and that was twenty years ago. I don't know what else to do. Oh well, nice to speak to Kath, now you have a lovely day tomorrow …' 'David wait,' said Kathleen. 'There is another way. I found a long-lost relative of mine and it doesn't have to involve solicitors or cost the earth. Have you tried the Salvation Army?' 'How can they help?' 'They run a family tracing service. Why don't you contact them?'

As soon as Christmas was over I followed Kathleen's

suggestion and rang the Salvation Army. 'How can we help you?' said a lady on the other end. I explained the nature of my enquiry. 'Right,' she said 'I'm going to put you through to Lieutenant Colonel Colin Fairclough; hold the line please.' The phone buzzed a couple of times before a man's voice answered. 'Colin Fairclough here – how can I help?' Again I went through the details of who I was and that I was looking for my birth relatives. Colin asked a few questions and wanted to know how much information I already had. I told him about finding the ad in the *Mercury* and that after that the trail had gone cold. 'The newspaper's records didn't go back to 1942, and anyway it was a confidential box number. It's just been so frustrating,' I said. Colin made understanding noises. It occurred to me he might have heard very similar stories many times over. 'Is your father's name on the birth certificate?' he asked. 'Because if not it could be difficult. The Salvation Army is in the business of bringing people together, not dragging skeletons out of the cupboard and tearing families apart.' I assured him my actual father's name was on the certificate. 'Good, then send us as much documentation as you can, a copy of the certificate and the press advertisement and any other information you have.' I gathered everything together as Colin had requested and posted it all off to the London address he had given me. I suddenly had a feeling of great impatience. Since finding that newspaper in Reading Library nearly forty years ago I had been up against a brick wall, as it were. Now for the first time in decades I had a glimmer of hope again, and it all seemed very exciting. Suppose the Salvation Army actually found I had another family somewhere! How would I feel on meeting them – what would they think about me? What stories might come tumbling out from the past! It was exciting, yes, but also terrifying in a way, and I was only too mindful of Colin's words about skeletons in cupboards. There was always a danger the sardine tin of my life with the little bit hidden in the corner could turn into Pandora's Box. It was Pandora's insatiable curiosity that had turned the whole world to darkness. But surely my curiosity was justified; how could simply uncovering the truth turn anyone's world to darkness?

I forced myself out of the house and into the cold January air. I had a fair bit of work on, paving and garden wall stuff. The weather was cold, though most days hovering just above freezing, allowing me to make some progress, and it was good to be back at it after the sloth and over-indulgence of Christmas. I decided to be patient with the Salvation Army and not expect a reply from them over-night, and they were after all doing it all for free. Finally I resigned myself to not hearing anything for several months at least, and was therefore surprised when, arriving home on the evening of 1 February, I found that a letter had arrived for me that morning. Seeing the London postmark I guessed it must be from the tracing service and tore open the envelope. Sure enough it was from Lieutenant Colonel Colin Fairclough. One sentence jumped out at me straight away:

Since receiving your letter we have carried out some research and believe that there may well be members of your family whom we could locate ...

Along with the letter was a questionnaire that I was asked to fill in and return as soon as possible. After we had had dinner I sat down and completed the questionnaire and posted it the very next morning. After all these years the brick wall had begun to break down, and I was now eager to see what would be revealed behind it. The communication from Colin had given me hope. It was very exciting to think I might be meeting relatives for the first time. There was also an element of anxiety. Supposing I met them and hated them on the spot? Or worse, what if they didn't want to know me?

15

In the second week of February 2002, I came home and saw another envelope with a London postmark lying on the mat. There was no way it could wait of course and I ripped it open immediately. It was from the Salvation Army. It read:

We have now received your completed enquiry form asking whether we might be able to trace any members of your family. You will be pleased to learn that we have found records of a son and daughter who were born to Ernest Henry Alfred Wort and Rose Lillian Wort. I have in fact had two conversations with the daughter and she in turn has held discussions with other members of the family. As you may well understand, they were unaware of your existence until I brought the matter to their attention. Because of this they are of course somewhat hesitant at this time about disclosing their addresses. They are however very keen to hear from you and to allow matters to develop in due course. The responses I have had from the family have been extremely positive …

This was encouraging, I thought. Extremely positive, it said. I knew the Salvation Army wouldn't paint a misleading picture. My worries about any relatives I found rebuffing me began to ease a little. What was more, it sounded like I had a brother and a sister. I found myself already wondering what they might be like. I continued reading Colin's letter:

… it has been suggested that to begin with you might care to write something about yourself (childhood, earliest memories, something of your present life and so on). This can then be sent to us and we will be happy to forward it on your behalf. The family would also be interested in having a photograph of you if you are able to supply this. I am able to say that Rose Lillian Violet Wort remarried after the war and has another son by that marriage.

So I had a half-brother too. My family was getting bigger by the minute! Colin's letter concluded on a note of caution:

… as you will fully understand we are dealing with extremely sensitive issues and a step-by-step approach to building a relationship is obviously indicated. We look forward to hearing from you shortly – and if you wish to call me any morning after 8.30am this week, then I shall be happy to discuss the matter further.

Yours sincerely,
Colin Fairclough Lieutenant Colonel
Director – Family Tracing Service

I sat in the armchair, re-reading the letter and turning over the information, and its implications, in my head. Should I ring now or later, I wondered. After a couple of hours I could wait no longer and was on the phone to Colin. 'What are their names ... how old are they ... where do they live ... are they married ... do they have children?' My questions were coming like machine-gun fire. Gently, Colin slowed me down to a gallop. 'You've got to understand,' he said calmly, 'your existence has come as a great shock to them. It's now up to them whether they go ahead and contact you or not.' He then went on to explain that in many cases families decided they didn't want to get in touch and that I should therefore not build my hopes up too high. He did say again though that having spoken twice to my sister, who he now told me was called Margaret, she seemed very positive. I wondered though how it was she'd never known of my existence. If our mother had not remarried till after the war, then maybe I'd been born the 'wrong side of the sheets'. Perhaps I was Rose's but not Ernest Wort's son, which would therefore make me Margaret's half-brother.

That evening I sat down and composed my letter of introduction to Margaret and my two brothers. This might sound a simple enough thing to do, but in fact it took a bit of thinking about. After all, it's not often you describe yourself and your way of life in such a way to complete strangers. How do you sum yourself up? I had to condense nearly sixty years of living into a couple of pages. In the end I decided it was best to keep it simple and not too long-winded, and got straight to the point. I opened by telling Margaret that I realised it must have come as a great shock to her and her family to discover they had a brother, or half-brother, whom they had never known of. I told her that, since I was now getting on for sixty, I thought it best to make a few enquiries, hence my approach to the Salvation Army. I enclosed a copy of a letter that I had already sent to the Salvation Army tracing service, and added a few extra details explaining how I had left school at fifteen and trained as a bricklayer, which had been my occupation ever since. I told her about my family, and my life-long enthusiasm for football. I also put in a photograph of myself, as Margaret had requested, together with some other documents. I concluded my letter by making clear that my enquiries had simply been to establish whether or not I had any living relatives, and that I wanted nothing from her or the family. I did add that I hoped we could meet in the near future.

On Monday, 25 February a letter arrived with a photograph enclosed. First I examined the picture closely. So, I thought, this is my brother, my own flesh and blood. I could see clearly we did look a bit alike. But what was he like as a person? I started to read the letter he had written to me:

Dear David,
There is so much to say that it is difficult to know where to begin ...

I know the feeling, I thought.

My name is Ian McEwan and I am your brother, your full brother. How this comes to be so I would rather tell you when we meet, which I hope will be soon. As you know, Margy and Roy (your half-sister and half-brother) and I knew nothing of your existence until we heard from the Salvation Army. The fact that we were never told about you is obviously a matter of sadness for us, but we are also very keen to meet you.

I was born in 1948 near Aldershot. Our father, David McEwan, was a Glaswegian who served in the army all his working life. (He died in 1996. His favourite younger brother by the way was called Stewart.) I grew up in various postings – Singapore, North Africa, Germany. At the age of eleven I was sent away to boarding school. I went to universities at Sussex and East Anglia. Early in the 1970s I started writing, and I've made my living as a novelist ever since.

I have two sons by my first marriage. The first is

eighteen and the second is almost sixteen and they have both lived with me these past few years. Also by my first marriage I have two stepdaughters, who are now in their late twenties and early thirties. I remarried in 1997. My wife is an editor who works on the *Guardian* newspaper.

Because Margy and Roy are so much older than me, I grew up rather like an only child. I always wanted a brother – and here you are, more than half a century late, but no less of a brother for that! Let's meet soon. I'll leave the next step to you. I'd prefer our first meeting to be one-to-one, but I'm happy to go along with whatever you'd like. Until then, very best wishes to you and your family.

16

I read Ian's letter over and over again. One of the first things that had struck me was that my name wasn't Wort after all. It was McEwan. So my father had been a Scotsman and I was half Scottish myself. Having enjoyed the numerous misfortunes of Scotland's football team over the years, discovering this part of my ancestry was a bit of a shock. It was like being told that having been a life-long Reading Football Club supporter I was in fact half a Swindon Town supporter. Swindon Town are Reading's traditional local rivals, and I'd be obliged to head west down the M4 every other Saturday to the county ground. But why had the name on my birth certificate been Wort? I looked out of the kitchen window at our first daffodils, which had that morning bared their yellow petals in the crisp February air. I have a little brother, I thought to myself. I wondered what he meant about being my full brother, and wanting to tell me more about this when we met. Well, there was only one way to find out. Where could we meet? He lived in Oxford, which wasn't far. There was a phone number on the letter. I thought it would be better to give him a ring in the afternoon; it would give me a chance to think what to say to the guy. It seemed strange saying it like that, proposing to speak to a brother whom I never knew I had for the first time ever, and at the age of nearly sixty. What the devil was I going to say to him? I couldn't do it, not straight away anyway.

In the event, however, I left it over the weekend, and the following Monday afternoon, having had more time to mull things over, I sat down, picked up the phone and dialled the number on the letter. 'Hello,' said a male voice. 'Could I speak to Ian McEwan please?' I said. 'Speaking,' said the voice. 'This is your brother David.' There was a long pause. 'Hello David,' he said at last. He then said how pleased he was to hear from me. I told Ian I had received his letter and was ringing to arrange a meeting as suggested. 'Do you know the Four Pillars Hotel at Sandford-on-Thames?' I asked. This was about equidistant between Oxford and my own home in south Oxfordshire. It was a large establishment and somewhere we could hopefully find a discreet corner in which to talk. Ian said this would be fine as a rendezvous point, and we made an appointment for 7.30pm on the coming Wednesday, 27 February, which, was in two days' time. We already both had snapshots so should have no trouble finding each other on the night. We then exchanged mobile phone numbers just in case, said goodbye and that was that. On the Wednesday afternoon I telephoned the Salvation Army to speak to Colin again. I'd been feeling a bit nervous and wanted to know what to expect when I met Ian. What were other people's experiences in this situation? 'Forget what you may have seen on television about family reunions' was Colin's advice. 'There will be no emotion. All you will do is fill in enormous voids in each other's lives. Good luck.' No emotion, well, I suppose that was true in one way. The problem was in not knowing what my emotions, if any, were going to be. What feelings are you likely to have about someone you're meeting for the first time? I realised I had been through nothing else in my life which compared with this forthcoming meeting and it was going to be a completely new experience for me. The same of course was true for Ian. We were both in the same boat in that respect at least.

On the Wednesday night I hurried my tea and had a quick shower, anticipating the evening ahead of me. I arrived at the Four Pillars at about 7.15pm and parked up. I walked into the large bar area of the hotel, bought a drink and sat down at a table facing the door. A few people arrived and the bar began to fill up, couples having an aperitif before dinner, small groups socialising and one or two business types. I looked at my watch. It was now just coming up to 7.30pm. It crossed my mind that our meeting may not be as important to Ian as it was to me, that he might even be squeezing me in between other appointments this evening.

The time came and went and I began to think Ian wasn't to show. When it got to 7.45pm I was just wondering if I should ring his mobile when a slim figure came through the main door and into the bar. I recognised him straight away, thinking that, as in his photograph, he looked a little bit like me. He spotted me looking at him and came over. 'Hello, I'm David,' I said standing up. 'Ian.' We shook hands and hugged very briefly. 'You're drinking sherry? May I get you another?' he said. 'No, no,' I said. 'That's not my glass – I'll have the house red.' Ian nodded and disappeared off to the bar. Looking over I saw him talking to someone, and assumed he'd bumped into an acquaintance. As I watched I saw the person produce a pen and paper and Ian wrote something. After a good ten minutes' wait Ian finally returned to our table with the drinks. Apparently the girl behind the bar was on her first day in the job, and being unable to open the wine bottle, and politely declining Ian's offer of help, had gone off to seek assistance from another member of staff. (Ian was to tell me later how agonising it had felt being delayed at the bar, with he and I having only just met, and for barely thirty seconds at that). Ian sat down and, as Colin had predicted, we began to fill in those 'enormous voids' in each other's lives. Ian showed me photographs of his wife and his sons from his first marriage. He also had a picture of our father, David McEwan. I peered closely at the face, studying the expression, trying to interpret it, to read something there. All I could think was that my father looked rather like prison officer McKay in

Porridge. 'I'm sorry to hear about our mother,' I said. Ian had already told me in his letter about Rose being in a nursing home, and that she was now suffering from vascular dementia. The burning question in my mind was still Ian's first comment in that letter, about telling me how we came to be brothers. 'I thought you knew nothing about me till I contacted you.' I said. 'Have you learned more since?' Ian went on to explain how, after they had received my letter, the family had got together to try to work out the circumstances surrounding my existence. What had happened between our parents all those years ago and why did nobody know of me or of the advert in the *Reading Mercury*? But someone did. Ian told me that when the family had sat down to discuss the matter, our Auntie Margie – Rose's sister – had come out with an extraordinary confession. Apparently Rose had still been married to Ernest Wort, with whom she already had two children, when she embarked on an affair with our father, Sergeant Major McEwan. That affair had resulted in Rose falling pregnant with me, and while Ernest was still away fighting in North Africa, she and my father had placed the ad in the *Reading Mercury*. The Sharps had been the first respondents and according to Auntie Margie, she and Rose had caught the train to Reading General Station where I was handed over to the other Rose, and her husband Percy, who were to become my mum and dad. The complete surrender had been executed. Mr and Mrs Sharp departed gratefully to Spring Terrace with their new charge and my mother Rose, having given birth to me just a few weeks earlier, hastened away empty-handed, never to hold me in her arms or see me again. Rose had sworn her sister to secrecy and Margie loyally carried that secret for sixty years. Ian told me that since revealing the truth Auntie Margie was cut up on two counts – firstly that she had now betrayed Rose's trust and secondly that she had been a party to casting me off and never letting me know about my real parents. 'So our parents registered my birth, but lied and for the certificate gave Ernest's surname as the father?' I said. Ian confirmed that this appeared to be the case. Gradually the puzzle was being pieced together. But had both parents been equally willing to give me up like some unwanted puppy? I couldn't believe any mother would do so without great distress. How had they discussed the matter, who had said what? The more answers I got only raised more questions.

Ian too had obviously learned a whole lot more about his parents since my appearance on the scene and Auntie Margie's subsequent revelation, information which it would no doubt take some time to process. Having known his mother and father all his life, it had turned out he didn't know them quite as well as he thought. Rose's husband had been injured in the D-Day landings and died shortly after from his wounds. This left Rose free, and in 1947 she and David McEwan got married, with Ian being born a year later. Apparently Rose's two children by Ernest – my half-brother and half-sister Margaret and Roy – as children had no part to play in our mother's second marriage. As Ian had told me in his letter, he'd spent much of his childhood on army bases around the world, returning to England and a state boarding school at age eleven. Ian said that my father was a sociable man who liked a drink and was very popular in the officers' mess. I also gathered that on certain occasions, after a convivial night out at the pub or the mess, he had been, shall we say, less than pleasant towards our mother. (Subsequent to this first meeting, Ian expressed concern that I should understand more fully this aspect of our father's behaviour, and his memories and reflections on these particular episodes within the family are detailed later in the book.) During the last few years of his life, a lung disease meant that my father became totally dependent on my mother. David McEwan, the father I never knew, had died in our mother's arms in 1996. Referring to the complete surrender advertisement offering me in the paper, Ian then remarked that it had 'our father's fingerprints all over it'. 'What do you mean, his fingerprints?' I asked. Ian explained that even if trying to find a home for a pet, one would write, 'loving home wanted', whereas when advertising me the wording had stated simply 'home wanted'. Ian commented that our father didn't express much love. (The distinction though between 'expressing love' and the existence of love was something else that Ian was keen to clarify to me later, stressing that in fact our father loved him 'fiercely'. This intense emotion was apparently sometimes a problem, due to our father being 'a dominating person', and Ian 'a rather timid child'.) Although I'd had those words from the newspaper burned into my mind for nigh on forty years, this underlying meaning, reading between the lines as Ian had now pointed out, had not entirely sunk in before. When looked at like that I suppose the advertisement did say something about the person behind the words. Ian had grown up with our father, so he should know.

Ian went on to ask me more about my own life now, my work and my hobbies. Well, work was work. The beautiful game on the other hand was something I could enthuse about. 'Football is still my passion,' I said. 'I did try to get in the Reading youth team many years ago.' Ian looked at me, nodding. Though he listened attentively it was plain he was not a fan. He confirmed he had no interest in football personally but told me that a friend of his did have a box at Old Trafford, to which he had been invited several times. So far he had not accepted the invitation. I did find it hard to believe that my brother, my own flesh and blood, had turned down the chance of sitting in a private box and whilst gorging on prawn sandwiches or whatever, watching Manchester United play football as well. It wasn't of course the only difference between us. I asked Ian about the person who'd been speaking to him earlier on the way to the bar. He said they had recognised him and asked for his autograph. Ian in his initial letter of introduction to me had already told me how for some years he had made his living as a novelist, though I'd never heard of him until then. Now I said, 'Well, for some years I have made my living as a bricklayer – had you heard of me at all?' We both laughed. From then on the questions and answers, the swapping of details and dates, likes and dislikes, the filling in of more of those gaps continued all evening. At one point I said, 'My story would make a good plot for one of your books.' Ian replied that it was my story, and I should write it. At 11pm we decided to call it a night and shook hands. Ian said he would be off to America in a few days to promote his new book *Atonement*, and would get in touch with me on his return if that would be all right. In fact, as I found out that evening, when I'd called him to arrange our meeting, Ian had been in the middle of an interview with journalists about the launch of this latest novel, and had taken the phone upstairs to continue our conversation in private.

It was nearly midnight when I got home. My mind was whirling with thoughts of the drama of wartime Britain, of fun-loving Rose (had she been?) and my father, the domineering Scottish Sergeant Major David McEwan, the life and soul of the bar room yet with a heart as cold as steel when need be. I thought too of poor young Ernest Wort – what was his story? And then I saw the two anxious sisters Rose and Margaret, wrapping up the tiny baby and bearing it to the train, and a childless couple waiting for the illicit rendezvous on a cold, desolate, windswept station. I thought of hope, fear, heartache, betrayal and regret.

17

On the 1 March a letter arrived from my half-sister Margaret. She introduced herself and said she had heard that Ian and I had met. She told me her husband's name was Eddie and between them they had three children and seven grandchildren. Eddie had been retired this past ten years and now they enjoyed the time they had to spend together. Margaret said she looked forward to us all being able to meet up in April, after their holidays, and closed with good wishes to me and my family, and expressing the hope that my 'expectations have not been shattered'. Since I'd had no specific expectations this was certainly not the case. I'd been surprised about certain revelations admittedly, but I was really still taking them all in I suppose. I did know I was delighted to discover from Margaret's letter that I was suddenly 'uncle' to so many nieces and nephews I had yet to meet.

The other person I had yet to meet of course was my

mother, Rose McEwan. Ian had told me that she was now eighty-six and that the nursing home in which she resided was in North Harrow. According to reports the vascular dementia had now severely impaired her memory, and some days she did not even recognise her daughter Margaret, who lived close by and visited her most days. However it is well known that in cases of dementia the sufferer's long-term memory is sometimes retained, with distant events being clearly recalled. Dare I hope that Rose may remember something of those events of 1942, something of me? However, even if this proved to be the case, would it be kind or prudent to jog that memory? I knew I had to tread carefully, both for my sake and hers. I wanted to see her, but the last thing I wanted was to distress an elderly lady. With Mothering Sunday coming up the following weekend my thoughts had turned to buying some flowers for my mum's grave. But I was also thinking of paying the other Rose a visit, Rose McEwan, my birth mother. But I couldn't just turn up. Perhaps I could phone the nursing home and make an appointment. But what was I going to say to them? It could be a bit of a shock all round. Maybe I could contact Margaret and see what she thought best. This seemed the best course of action. So on the Friday evening prior to Mothering Sunday I phoned my half-sister's number. When I got through to Margaret's place a man answered. 'I'm sorry,' he said. 'Margaret's not in. Who's calling?' 'This is David,' I said. 'I'm her half-brother. Margaret and I have been in touch.' The man was, as I'd assumed, Eddie,

Margaret's husband. 'I'd like to go and see Rose,' I explained, 'and thought I'd better ring Margaret to discuss the best way to go about it. I understand Rose is unwell and not herself these days. I was thinking of perhaps seeing her on this coming Mothering Sunday.' Eddie explained that Margaret was presently staying down in Cornwall, visiting the Eden Project. 'I'll give her a call and ring you back,' he said. Within the hour Eddie called back and a plan was arranged. Margaret would not be returning before Mothering Sunday, so on the day I was to travel up to their house and meet Eddie, who would take me on to the nursing home.

When the day came I drove up to North Harrow alone. I felt it best that for this first visit at any rate, it should be just me seeing Rose. I didn't want to overwhelm the poor woman with strange faces. I could perhaps take other people with me on future occasions. During the drive I pondered the question of how I should introduce myself. I couldn't possibly say 'Hello Rose, I'm your son' – could I? Mauville House produced an in-house magazine, of which Margaret had kindly given me the Spring 2001 edition. For this edition my brother Ian had written a short history of our mother's life, recording that after our father retired from the army he and Rose had returned to live in her childhood home of Ash. There, her pride and joy had been her beautiful garden, where she had grown tulips, her favourite flower. Therefore the previous day I had gone in to the florists and bought the best white tulips in the shop, to present to Rose when I met her after our near sixty years' separation. I arrived at Eddie and Margaret's house where Eddie and I shook hands and exchanged pleasantries. The thought crossed my mind that when my half-sister returned the first thing she was going to ask her husband was 'Well, what's he like?' and I wondered how Eddie was going to describe me. Mauville House, the home where Rose resided was just a short drive away. As we drew up in front of its net-curtained windows, Mauville reminded me rather of a seaside guesthouse and I almost expected to see a 'No Vacancies' sign displayed somewhere. Walking up to the entrance Eddie rang the bell, explaining as he did so that the doors to the home were always kept locked. Most of the residents were apparently in a similar mental condition to Rose, and if any of them found an open door they had no hesitation in taking a breath of fresh air and wandering off down the street. Rose, Eddie confided, was 'chair of the home's escape committee' and had let herself out on a couple of occasions when doors had been left inadvertently unbolted. A male manager, who I got the impression was Irish, greeted us and showed us into a comfortable carpeted lounge with several wing armchairs arranged around. Some of the elderly residents, most of them ladies, were dozing, while others talked with visitors. In the corner a large television set dominated the room, its constant chatter and flickering screen largely ignored by most of those present. To me, at that particular moment, there seemed a terrible air of sadness, in some ways only made worse by the obvious efforts to brighten things up. The huge TV, the shiny ornaments, the quiet, dutiful conversation of the relatives were all well-meaning and nicely done, but couldn't dispel my overriding sense of pity for the poor souls whose lives were now dwindling to an end here. 'God's waiting room' summed it up. The manager then returned and said, 'Would you like to come with me?' He took us along a corridor, knocked on a door and opened it. 'Rose,' he said, 'you've got some visitors – your son-in-law Eddie and another gentleman – I'll go and fetch you all a cup of tea.' Sitting in an armchair was a very small white-haired lady. She looked up as we entered. 'Hello love, how are you today?' said Eddie. 'Here's David come to see you.' I looked at Rose, and she looked back at me. For the first time ever I was face to face with the woman who had given birth to me nearly sixty years ago. Still looking at me she said, 'Oh hello Uncle, I wondered when you were coming.' I hesitated for a moment, not knowing what response to make. At that point I felt no emotion, only sorrow for the present state of mind of this dear old lady whose room and life I had just sauntered into. I walked over and held out the bunch of tulips. 'I brought you these, I was told you like them,' I said. On seeing the flowers her face transformed, lighting up in a warm smile, her soft eyes twinkling. 'Oh I love tulips,' she said. 'I grow them in my garden.' I laid the tulips on the bedside cabinet. 'Do you mind if I sit with you?' I said. Rose seemed to assent, so I sat down next to her on the bed. 'Well, how are things? It's a lovely day today, isn't it?' I remarked in a light-hearted voice, at the same time cursing myself I couldn't think of something more original to say. Rose looked at me again then said in a bright voice, 'I'm going home soon. I hope the house is still clean, I left everything clean.' I smiled and nodded, hoping I didn't seem to be patronising her. Perhaps it might help the conversation if we did something together. 'Do you mind if I have my picture taken with you?' I asked Rose. She nodded, seeming pleased at the idea. I moved closer and we both did our best 'cheeses' as Eddie took a couple of photographs. There were so many things I wanted to ask the old lady, so much I wanted to say. I told her a little bit about myself, where I lived and about my family. I then asked her, 'How many children did you have Rose?' She looked thoughtful for a moment. As I held my breath she replied, 'Six.' I did a quick calculation in my head – could it be she was remembering something? Margaret, Roy, David, Ian and two others – might she be including me in this list of her offspring? Thinking 'in for a penny in for a pound' I said, 'Who were those six then, what were their names?' Rose then promptly reeled off six names. I knew none of them. I looked at Eddie. The names she'd given he said were those of her carers here at the home. As I'd originally been given the name Stewart David, which the Sharps had turned around, I then said carefully, 'Do you remember anything about Stewart?' She looked at me steadily and vaguely moved her head. Was that a yes, a no or complete incomprehension? I smiled and murmured politely. Cups of tea arrived and we began to chat about general topics, the weather, plants and

Two advertisements which were to mark such important points in my life: *above*, the original advertisement that appeared in the *Reading Mercury* on 12 December 1942, which lead to my biological parents successfully giving me away and *left*, the advert that I placed at the start of my quest to find my true parents.

Outside the house where I grew up and *inset*, some sixty years earlier, outside the same house, the summer that I arrived, aged nine months, in my battered old pram.

Above: Taken on Mothering Sunday, I am sat with my mother, Rose, for the first time. Moments before this photo was taken she had mistakenly called me 'uncle'.

Below: With my mother's two sisters: my aunties Joan (*right*) and Margie, who accompanied my mother and me to Reading Station all those years ago.

When I began the search for my real family, the thought that I might discover a brother hadn't once crossed my mind. Here, I sit with Ian McEwan, my younger, full brother.

gardens, how we liked our tea. From the outside, the scene must have looked very calm, with no hint of the thoughts and questions that were tumbling around in my head as the grey-haired old lady who had given birth to me conversed blithely and amicably with the child she had surrendered all those years ago. All too soon, it was time to go. 'It's been lovely to see you,' I said. I stood up from the bed and kissed her goodbye, thinking, I have touched this face before. She would have kissed me then too, surely. But I wondered, at the railway station as she held me out to the waiting arms of a stranger, had she bent and given her tiny child one last kiss goodbye? I could not believe she wouldn't have cried. At the door I looked back at Rose's delicate silvered head and kindly smiling face, and meditated yet again at the secret of me she had kept hidden for well over half a century. During all those years had she ever thought about me and how I was getting on, pondered on what I looked like, and whether I was well? I felt she must have done, but how would I ever know that for sure?

Driving home down the M40 I was filled with an intense sadness. I thought back over the visit I had just made, and tried to analyse the reason for my distress. Apart from natural pity for Rose and her state of mind, the fact was I couldn't also help feeling that by going to see her I had somehow betrayed my mum and dad. They had given me a home, brought me up and never stopped loving me. They had given me everything in fact. Rose McEwan, or Rose Wort as she had been when she bore me, had given me nothing.

This may not have been her fault, and who was I or anyone else to judge the actions of a person half a century ago and in wartime too. For all I knew the act may have caused her deep unhappiness. I couldn't get the image of Mum and Dad out of my head though. There was a sense I had violated something that had previously been pure, the innocence of their love for me, and that having stepped out of that perfect triangle of love to admit the other Rose, I had somehow cracked the mould. It seemed to me that Mum and Dad must know what I had done, that I had committed this act of ingratitude, and the feelings of guilt and disloyalty wouldn't go away. By the time I arrived back home however my mood had lifted somewhat, and I began to see the situation in a more positive light. Look what I had gained – after being an 'only child' all my life I now had one full brother, a half-brother and a half-sister, two sisters-in-law, a brother-in-law and a whole load of nieces and nephews whom hopefully I would soon have the pleasure of meeting. When my half-sister Margaret returned from Cornwall she and I spoke over the phone and discussed when and where we should get together. We set the date of Sunday, 28 April, and agreed it would be nice to have lunch. Arrangements were made for us to meet up at a restaurant near Margaret and Eddie's place; here I would meet my half-sister Margaret and husband Eddie and half-brother Roy and his wife Merle. So far my half-brother Roy was the only one of my three siblings who had not communicated with me, and I thought that maybe he'd only been talked into attending this forthcoming meeting by Margaret, and maybe Merle. I hoped he and I would get on, but knew that only time would tell. On the day, Eddie was waiting at the door of the restaurant as I pulled into the car park. He led the way in and did the introductions. As soon as I saw Roy I was amazed at how much he looked like me. We all shook hands, sat down and chatted as we studied the menu. Margaret had organised the seating plan and I was between Roy and Merle. Roy and I soon had plenty to talk about since it was obvious we shared a love of football, he being a season-ticket holder at his local club Woking. When the meals arrived at our table the convivial conversation continued and everyone seemed to be having a good time. Talking about the event afterwards, Margaret was to describe the food in the restaurant as 'crap'. If at that point I'd been in any doubt about us being related, this comment would have convinced me. But the standard of cuisine was hardly the issue, the opportunity for us to meet together as a family was what was important. One thing in particular I took away with me that afternoon was something my half-brother Roy confided to me. 'My son said it'd be a waste of time coming here today, and I agreed with him,' he said. 'But now I'm glad I came to meet you, you're just an ordinary guy like me.' Thanks Roy, I thought, an 'ordinary guy' is all I've ever wanted to be.

Now I had met more members of my birth family I felt pleased and fortunate that they had accepted me and that we had all got on in such a friendly fashion. It could have so easily gone the other way I thought, remembering Colin at the Salvation Army warning me about the possibility that I might be rejected. It seemed so terribly sad that my mother Rose and I could not communicate over the most important thing that bound us together, the giving of life. On the other hand, although her condition was tragic and painful for her loved ones, perhaps the fact that she was oblivious of who I was could be looked on as a blessing in some ways.

There was now only one person, a key player in the unfolding drama of my early life, who had still not made an appearance. It was the person who, on the day I was given away, had accompanied my mother and me every step of the way to that fateful rendezvous. Where was Auntie Margie?

18

If Muhammad won't come to the mountain, then the mountain, as they say, has to go to Muhammad. Auntie Margie had become my Muhammad. I knew she was living in the UK within easy reach, and of course she now knew that I was aware of the basic facts about how she and my mother had surreptitiously handed me over as a baby at the Reading Railway Station in 1942. In fact it was she who had so recently told all this to the rest of the family. But I had still not met her or received any direct communication from her. Though obviously elderly herself she was apparently in reasonable possession of her faculties. Bearing in mind her age I could understand her not being present at the lunch meeting with Roy and Margaret, but presumably she could contact me, either by phone, letter or message, via the family if she wished. Perhaps she felt I had no interest in meeting her, or that I might be resentful about what had happened, and the fact she'd kept it a secret all these years. Possibly the thought of a direct encounter between us was simply too nerve-wracking at her time of life. I wondered if I should respect that and leave her in peace, rather than pester an old lady just to satisfy my curiosity. But was she in peace? Or were the events of sixty years ago, especially now I was in the know, a burden which she longed to unload? Partly she'd done that by telling the family. Nevertheless I was the crucial element in what she had colluded in, and now especially, my existence must surely be playing on her mind. So long as it was in a spirit of friendship and reconciliation, maybe she would welcome my making the first move. With this in mind I decided to let Auntie Margie know that I'd like us to meet, and rather than approach her directly I duly passed the message on through my half-sister Margaret. After all, nothing ventured, nothing gained, and my aunt could only say no.

She did. My half-sister Margaret came on the phone a few days after I'd put in my request. 'I'm sorry David,' she said, 'but Auntie Margie just doesn't want to meet you.' 'Why?' I asked. 'Well, she feels very embarrassed by all this.' These words were, to say the least, disappointing. But I shouldn't have been altogether surprised. Sixty years was a long time ago, a long time to keep a secret. I remembered my dad's words when I'd questioned him about getting me out of a paper: 'It's water under the bridge son.' Now, Reading Railway Station 1942 was even further behind us in the long river of history. Maybe if enough water goes under a bridge, that bridge, linking the present to the past, gets washed away. My thoughts also went back to what Lieutenant Colonel Colin Fairclough of the Salvation Army had told me when I had first telephoned him. 'It's up to them whether they decide to meet you or not. You will need a very thick skin. They may reject you.' It was up to Auntie Margie. I had put the ball in her court, and she had decided to keep it there. Well, she had if you like 'come clean' regarding my existence when asked by other members of the family, so maybe that was enough for her. Even if that were so, and she felt entirely at peace over the matter, which frankly I doubted, it wasn't enough for me. I desperately wanted to meet with her. There were so many questions I wanted to ask, so many things I needed to know. Auntie Margie had all the answers. 'How about this,' I said to Margaret. 'What if I write a letter to Auntie Margie and you pass it on?' Margaret obviously couldn't guarantee that my auntie would reply, but agreed to my request. I therefore sat down, composed my thoughts and began to write, thinking carefully about the effects my words would have on her. The completed letter ran as follows:

Dear Auntie Margaret,

I am writing to introduce myself. My name is David Sharp but you probably remember me (hopefully) as Stewart, the baby Rose gave away almost sixty years ago. Sixty years ago the world was completely different to the one we live in now. Things happened during the war that probably wouldn't happen now. I would like to say how much I admire you for supporting Rose at a most difficult time in her life and for her benefit keeping my existence secret all these years. No one could have asked more from their sister. As it turned out I had a very happy childhood and I do not have any animosity, nor do I blame anyone for events that happened all those years ago. I'm just happy to have found my brothers and sister after all these years. Auntie Margaret, I am part of your family and I would very much like to meet you. It probably came as a shock when you heard I had made contact with Margaret through the Salvation Army but, as I stated earlier in this letter, I have nothing but admiration for you in your support of my mother. I hope you look on my request to meet you favourably. If you decide for any reason that you don't wish to meet me I'll abide by your decision and wish you a happy and healthy future. I am giving this letter to Margaret to pass on to you.

God Bless.
David

Hoping ardently that this would change my auntie's mind, I sealed the envelope, stuck on a first-class stamp and, on 27 August 2002, dropped the letter in the letterbox. For the next few days I tried to keep my mind occupied on work and other matters.

A week went by and there was no reply from Auntie Margie. I became impatient and then despondent. After nearly a fortnight had gone by I was convinced she did not want to see me. The letter had been my best shot; it had been, I hoped, honest yet as carefully designed as possible not to alarm or upset her in any way, and made it clear how very keen I was to meet. I couldn't force the issue and there seemed nothing more I could try. One day in mid September, however, I had just got in from work when the phone rang. It was Margaret. 'Hello David, I've been speaking to Auntie Margie and she has changed her mind. She would like to meet you after all.' I still don't know whether it was my letter that had influenced Auntie Margie, or whether the family had coerced her into seeing me. Maybe a bit of both – I hoped my letter had played some part. The main thing was that we were to meet.

The get-together was arranged to take place at the home of her daughter Jackie and her husband Peter in Farnham, Surrey. At long last I was going to meet someone who had been an eyewitness to the first few weeks of my life, and who could give me the true details of the events leading up to my being given away at one month old.

Auntie Margie was born on the 19 June 1919. At the age of twenty she married her husband John (everybody called him Jack) in 1939. In 2001 Margie and Jack celebrated their sixty-second wedding anniversary. Sadly, Jack passed away shortly afterwards. On more than one occasion during our conversation, Auntie Margie was to confide in me just how very much she missed him.

I walked into Jackie and Peter's comfortable lounge where, amidst other relatives, sat a lady with silver-white hair, bearing a strong resemblance to my mother. 'I've had a sleepless night worrying about meeting you,' she said. She looked at me apprehensively. 'I'm so glad you changed your mind about that,' I replied. 'There are so many things about me that I'd like to know.' She did not answer this comment. Instead, whether through nerves or what I don't know, but she proceeded to tell me in great detail about how ill-fitting her new teeth were and how the summer heat made her ankles swell. After a minute or two of this chitchat however she looked directly at me, and with a twinkle in her eye said, 'David, I've seen you with no clothes on.' Here I am, I thought, nearing sixty and in a room full of relatives I've only just met and she hits me with that! How could I answer? I looked straight back at her and ventured, 'Auntie Margie, I can honestly say I've not changed one little bit.' And from then on that was that, and we talked freely and comfortably. The ice between us was broken.

Amazingly after so many years, my auntie's memory seemed quite clear about the events that took place all those distant years ago. 'I used to push you round the streets of Aldershot most afternoons,' she said. Did this mean that my mother had shuffled me off into the care of her sister as soon as I was born? As far as she knew, went on Auntie Margie, her sister Joan, Joan's husband Eric, and her own late husband Jack had been the only ones in the family who knew of my existence. Apparently my mum and dad's response to the *Reading Mercury* advertisement had been the first to drop through the letterbox. Rose, my mother, worried in case the couple changed their minds, wrote back to the Sharps immediately to say that they could have me. The *Mercury* did apparently forward several other letters, but these were all put to one side, and after the handover they were destroyed. It had been agreed with the Sharps that I would be given away at Reading Railway Station just before Christmas. The sisters set out with me in the morning to catch the train, and apparently the day got off to a bad start. Not only was the December weather cold and drizzly, but the train was also late. This couldn't have helped the mood of the two women, my mother especially. When the train did arrive, I had shown my disapproval of the situation, recalled Auntie Margie, by screaming non-stop all the way to Reading. It was nice to know that I had expressed an opinion at any rate. Auntie Margie said, 'I told her: "You've still got a chance to change your mind Rose." But Rose was adamant – what had to be done had to be done was all she kept insisting.' I wondered, was she simply under immense pressure from my father to dispose of me as quickly as possible? One particular question had been nagging at me ever since I'd known about the handover. 'Since you and Rose had never met the Sharps,' I said, 'how did know when you got to the station that you were giving me away to the right people?' Auntie Margie explained that the procedure had been prearranged in letters between my mother and my mum and dad. After getting off the train, Rose and Margie would wait for the other passengers to disperse. The Sharps were then to approach them, the thinking being that there wouldn't be more than one pair of women on the platform holding a small baby. The assumption proved correct, and when the steam and passengers from the incoming locomotive had cleared, the Sharps walked straight over to Rose and Margie. Auntie Margie said that when it came to the actual moment of giving me away, she 'couldn't bear it'. Knowing that Rose was about to place her baby in the hands of complete strangers and say goodbye to him for the very last time, Margie was filled with emotion. 'I couldn't stand to watch. Although you were only a month old, you were part of my life as well as your mother's. I tried to reason with her one last time but still she wouldn't listen. As the strangers approached I had to walk away up the platform and turn my face away.'

As well as me, my mother had brought along a brown paper carrier bag, stuffed full of my baby clothes. What happened next, according to Auntie Margie, took no more than a couple of minutes. After my noisy screaming on the train, the whole operation on that cold December day must have been over and done with in little more time than it would have taken my mother to buy the train tickets.

Afterwards, on the face of it at least, it seemed everybody was happy. My mother could continue with her life as before and my mum, who by this time, as I learned, had had three miscarriages, now at long last had the baby she had so desperately longed for. 'But on the way back home I kept asking Rose why she had done such an awful thing,' said Auntie Margie. 'All she would say was "I just had to, I just had to", over and over again.' On that journey back from Reading my mother made her sister swear never to tell anyone of the events of that day. Margie had kept that promise for nearly sixty years, only disclosing the truth after I had started to make enquiries.

What, I wondered, of the other letters to the paper from those offering me a home? Were they all couples similarly desperate for a baby, or were there some whose agenda was more sinister maybe? Thoughts of Hyndley and Brady surfaced again, not to mention Fred and Rosemary West. How lucky I was to have been taken in by two people who gave me everything they could, materially and emotionally.

One thing about the whole episode did make me smile. Auntie Margie told me that when the plan for my handover at Reading Station was set, she had knitted me a special little outfit for the occasion. With the war on wool was in short supply, and the only colours she could get hold of were white and royal blue. She'd therefore knitted my going-away suit in a pattern of blue and white hoops. Unbelievable I thought; just one month old and about to be jettisoned into an unknown future, and I'm already wearing Reading colours. I wonder what happened to the little blue and white outfit. Now that would be a souvenir!

19

The little village of Ash in Surrey is close to Aldershot, traditionally the home of the British Army. The countryside around Ash bears witness to the encroachment of human beings and the changes in architectural fashions — and priorities — over the years. The most dominant type of housing around Ash goes back a few decades to the late sixties and seventies, the kind of sprawling estates built by the likes of Wimpeys and Wates — the 'Acacia Avenues' and 'Dryden Closes', with big picture windows, open-plan L-shaped lounges and reasonably generous-sized gardens, front and back. Room to breathe and to grow a neighbourhood. As Churchill once said, 'We shape our buildings and then they shape us.' With the exception of some solid Victorian cottages and terraces, there doesn't seem to be a great deal of other residential development in Ash till you go back several hundred years to the ancient, wobbly-walled and thatched cottages. Passing the address next door to St Peter's Church in Ash, I stop to read the plaque on the wall of one such Olde Worlde home, 'Hartshorne Cottage', dated circa 1350 AD. How much human coming and going, over all those centuries, this house must have seen. How many changing seasons it must have witnessed. What a succession of kings and queens, announcements, quarrels, bloodshed, disease, love, marriage, feasting, rituals, secrets overheard, death and rebirth, a rich brocade of English history, was stored deep within its ancient timbers. Its doorway seems tiny, a reminder that the average person was much shorter hundreds of years ago. Looking at old suits of armour you realise most of those gallant knights of yore were no taller than Ronnie Corbett. Ash is clearly a place that prides itself on preserving its links to the past. Adjacent to the cottage and linked to St Peter's by the cemetery to the rear is a comparatively large old building signposted as 'Ash Museum'.

Ash village is about to mark one particular occasion in its, and my own, history. Having driven down on a cold day, Friday, 9 January 2004, I am here to attend the funeral of my birth mother, Rose McEwan.

Passing through the gate of the churchyard I make my way between two rows of stout yew trees and enter the old timber-framed porch. Organ music can be heard playing softly within. Inside the church, the weak January sun filters through the stained-glass windows, picking out a million dust particles engaged in a never-ending dance through time and space. Earth to earth, dust to dust, ashes to ashes. Several of the family are already here, being ushered to the front pews, which have been reserved for close relatives. Walking over cast-iron grilles, probably originally housing under-floor heating before the heavy old radiators were installed, I find my place and nod quietly to acquaintances, reflecting on the fact that I am now surrounded by people who a few short months ago I would have passed in the street without a second glance, but that I now know as my family. It is a family that hitherto had known nothing of my existence. Apart, that is, from one person, a person who had vowed never to divulge the secret of my birth, Aunt Margaret. And now we are all gathered together to enact a ritual that is played out in thousands of families every year, a funeral for one of its senior members.

Glancing round the church, I notice that a woman seated behind us, whom I do not know, is staring intently at me. The vicar, the Reverend Haydock Wilcox, welcomes everyone and bids us be upstanding for the first hymn.

'All things bright and beautiful, all creatures great and small,

All things wise and wonderful, the Lord God made them all ...'

The words take me back to my days in the choir, and I remember singing it at school too: '... the rich man at his castle, the poor man at his gate, he made them high and lowly and ordered their estate ...' Glancing across at my brother Ian, I can't help wondering, did the good Lord order our particular estates? Ian is a supporter of the British Humanist Association. Presumably he wouldn't describe our differing circumstances in terms of being divinely ordained in any way. How then? I wonder. During the singing I feel sure that the woman behind is looking at me again.

When the hymn is finished we kneel for a short prayer, after which Ian ascends to the pulpit. He is going to speak about his mother, our mother, about her life. The eulogy he delivers is both informative and moving. Our mother was born in 1915, just up the road from the church in which we were now standing, at Number 2 Smiths Cottages. Ian describes the world that our mother came into, a rural community where life revolved around the seasons and the needs of farming. Apart from the little railway station at Ash Vale, transport was mostly of the horse-drawn variety when our mother was growing up. Ian mentions a photo of her with her father in uniform, one of the fortunate survivors of the Great War. Our mother was the eldest of five children, four girls and one boy. Her father's peacetime trade was that of house painter. My maternal granddad and I have something loosely in common then I suppose, me being a brickie. Our mother didn't have it easy as a girl and being the eldest had to shoulder responsibility for her siblings. Money and food being scarce she suffered from malnutrition and had to wear callipers for a period. Ian emphasises that later on our mother was by contrast very fit and healthy, cycling long distances down to the coast and back, swimming and walking for miles. He talks about her first job, which, as for many girls in those days, was in service as a chambermaid. Then comes her marriage to Ernie Wort, and his early death from battle injuries at Nijmegen. Apparently our mother travelled to see him in the hospital in Daventry before he died. A new phase of our mother's life begins. At this point I expect to get glances from some of the mourners, this being roughly the date at which I enter the recently revised family history. From the corner of my eye I can see the woman who was staring earlier. Now her face seems to be deliberately turned away. Everyone is concentrating on Ian, who is outlining our mother's remarriage after the war and her life as a mother and officer's wife travelling around the world. Ian focuses on all her positive attributes, her home-making and feminine skills, her delicious cooking, expert needlework and knitting, and hand-made gifts of woollen jackets for babies. At the same time our mother was no mere stay-at-home wife and mum, and whilst abroad learnt to shoot with a .22 rifle and won medals. She was also it seems an excellent dancer and in her sixties trained and worked as a librarian with the British forces in Germany. Ian is painting a vivid picture of Rose for us, one with which many of those present in the church today are familiar, and they nod in gentle accord as their fond remembrances of a dear departed mother, aunt or grandmother are here and there stirred. Others of us are still learning about Rose and the life she led, the vibrant, varied person that she was. For my picture of our mother I must rely largely on Ian and my half-siblings. They too of course have learned something of her from me, albeit indirectly. That something has no place here today. Ian's eulogy is just that, a speech of gratitude and a tribute to the woman who brought him up and whom he loved. A girl from humble origins who became the lively, elegant army wife, gaily fox-trotting her way around the colonies in the twilight years of the Empire, a woman of accomplishments, a wife and mother who cared for and counselled her children and nursed her sick husband to his dying day.

But as Ian's measured tones resonate around the church, I find myself thinking about the others in our mother's story; my half-siblings Roy and Margaret. Where did they figure exactly, and how truly happy was my mother and father's marriage? And where the dickens does this smartly attired brickie sitting in the front pew fit in? To be fair the vicar has already itemised all Rose's children and included me amongst them, so at least I'm on the list, a mention in dispatches if you like, and most people in the congregation will know who I am by now. And Ian, having mentioned none of our mother's children by name in his oration, has certainly not excluded me. But inevitably, from a personal point of view, sitting in the church on this particular occasion, I feel as if I'm here, yet not here really, acknowledged, but not in the official biography of our mother. I am an appendix or a subplot. I suppose this is how the untidy aspects of any person's life should be, on the occasion of their leaving this world.

Ian has now moved on to our mother's artistic side. Her secret pastime he says was writing poetry and she once read Ian a long piece inspired by a vision she'd had whilst under anaesthetic. In this poem she had described walking down a tunnel of light towards heaven where she met her father. He turned her back because her time had not yet come. Ian, who seems to be coming to the end of his eulogy, is now saying that our mother '... once told Merle, with all the authority that befits a mother-in-law, that the journey from heaven to earth takes three days. That means she will have got in at about 5.30 on the 29th December. I'm sure we all wish that she's comfortably installed.' There is a murmur of appreciation for Ian's words. The vicar thanks him and announces, 'We will now sing the final hymn in your order of service, "The Lord is My Shepherd" ... '

After the final prayers, some people remain kneeling. Others are already drifting in ones and twos towards the door. There is some low, respectful murmuring, odd snippets of conversation about who's parked where and the offering of lifts. I sit looking at the small wooden coffin resting on the trestles in front of the altar. What am I feeling? My own emotions are hard to gauge. Mostly I'm sorrowful for the relatives here today who knew Rose as a mother, aunt or grandmother all their lives, for Ian. Today especially, Rose is his mother not mine. I feel too for my half-brother Roy and particularly for my half-sister Margaret, who visited our mother most days, witnessing helplessly the steady decline of our mother from the vascular dementia, destroying so remorselessly the person she loved. For myself I do not have that sense of grief that a son should naturally experience at his mother's passing. But then, my mum died nearly forty years ago. The frail lady laying here in the coffin, a lady whom I'd met just a few times before today, was someone else. Then I catch my breath, remembering again that Rose McEwan and I had of course first met sixty years ago. She was my mother, she must have held me in her arms then, kissed me, loved me, then. Can a woman give birth and truly ever forget the person she has given life to? Only a mother could answer that. When I was a child my mother was never there to pick me up and 'kiss it better' when I fell over. Did she ever wonder if I was alive or dead, or think of me on my birthdays? Did she ever have the urge to try to seek me out during all those lost years? As I had lived in the same house for the first quarter century of my life I guess the answer had to be no. Though how could I be sure? If she had been 'herself' during our recent meetings in the care home, what secrets might she have told me? And what would she have thought of my existing family? What a lot we all missed out on. I suppose there are 'if onlys' in everyone's life. For me — if only confidences had been broken, if only my biological parents had tried to contact me, if only I had made more effort earlier on to seek them out. On the other hand, what would Mum and Dad have felt about that? Mum in particular, I know, would have been heartbroken. A child cannot have two mothers. Thinking again about whether my mother may have tried to keep in touch with me, I recall something Kathleen, who'd lived with us as an evacuee in Spring Terrace, had told me recently. She recounted how, on my first birthday, she had seen my mum open a card that had arrived at the house. 'She read the card,' said Kathleen, 'then tore it into tiny fragments and threw it on the fire.' Still wondering, I look again at Rose's coffin and think about the two women who had met, so very briefly, on a railway station all those years ago.

Following the service the mourners adjourned a short distance to the Hays and Jarvis Hotel, still better known to many as the old Hogs Back Hotel. After a few minutes milling around among the assembled company, I felt a slight tug on my arm. I turned to see a lady standing next to me. At a guess I'd say she was about twenty years younger than myself. I'd seen her before. It was the lady who'd been looking at me during the funeral service. She introduced herself. 'I'm your cousin, Dorothy,' she said. 'Oh – how do you do,' I said. 'I'm David.' 'Yes,' she said, 'I know. Listen, I'm sorry for staring at you in the church earlier, it's just that I was unprepared.' 'Unprepared?' I said. 'Yes, for the uncanny resemblance. You look so much like my uncle, your father. And you look like my father too,' she said. Her parents, she told me, had been my father's brother, George and his wife Nancy. Dorothy said that she and her husband Mark had come over from Ireland for the funeral, and were staying in London overnight with Ian. 'When Ian told me about you I was completely taken aback,' she went on. 'Partly because I couldn't understand why Rose and David hadn't tried to find you after they had married. Also I couldn't understand my auntie, Rose, doing something like that – a child out of wedlock? It just doesn't fit her image.' Hearing this I made no reply, but the expression on my face must have said it all.

I think Ian, who was standing nearby, also understood it. 'These days it's acceptable I suppose,' Dorothy continued, 'but back then it was all about disgrace to the family.' Dorothy gave me a brief outline of her life. Her mother was born in Fife, before moving to Edinburgh as a child and leaving school at fourteen. Her mother's first job was in the printing trade, until joining the Women's Royal Air Force just prior to the start of World War II. Dorothy's mother then met and married my father's brother George in Edinburgh in 1956, and later moved to Glasgow, where she still resides, in the Govan area. George had died a few years previously. I realised that, with my father having had so many siblings, there was probably a lot more to learn about my extended birth family's history, stretching down the years and connecting me at last with people like my cousin Dorothy. What Dorothy told me next though particularly caught my interest. 'I haven't yet told my mum that she has another nephew,' she said. 'Ian seems to think she may have known about you, but I'm not so sure myself.' Hmmm, I thought, my Aunt Nancy is someone I'd dearly like to meet in that case. Even if she hadn't known Rose and David's big secret, she could probably tell me a lot of other things about them.

To be honest I can't remember whether I was invited or whether I invited myself, but a couple of months after my mother's funeral I caught a flight up to Glasgow to pay a visit to my newly found Auntie Nancy. A couple of friends of Nancy met me at the airport, and as we drove through Govan I looked around at the buildings, trying to work out how similar it still was to how it had been when my father lived there. They say old stones retain memories. Did the stones of Govan remember my father walking these same streets, seeing what I was seeing now?

Nancy, though in the twilight years of her life, had a mind as sharp as a pin. Over a pot of tea, she talked to me about my mother and father, and in particular their visits to Glasgow, made while my father was still serving in the army. It had turned out that she hadn't known about me, though she did know other things about my parents, and there was one specific anecdote I found hard to credit, or even to comprehend at first. It concerned a visit made by my parents when Ian was still quite little, about six or seven years of age. During this visit, said Aunt Nancy, Rose and David were in a fractious, unhappy mood, and my father in particular seemed very angry about something. 'Did they say what the matter was?' I asked. 'Yes. It turned out they had been attempting to adopt a child. When I heard this my jaw almost dropped onto my tea plate. 'Adopt?' I exclaimed. 'Say that again would you, Aunt Nancy?' 'Well, you see they'd been trying for another baby, but for some reason Rose was unable to have one. So they'd been looking to adopt one.' Well, well, I thought, what about that. 'So why was my father so fired up about this when he came to see you? I asked. 'Because he'd just been told by the army that they wouldn't allow it – they refused to let him and Rose adopt a child. They'd applied for permission several times, but David's superiors wouldn't have it. And when they came to see me that day, they'd just been turned down again. The army seemed quite adamant about the matter and wouldn't budge in their decision. David was really furious about the whole situation.' Could the army do that, I wondered, prevent one of their men adopting a child? Presumably they could in this case. But what was it that had prompted them to intervene in my parents' domestic affairs? Perhaps it was simply some technicality to do with the provision of army quarters or Queen's regulations. If not, then had the military authorities had reservations about Rose and David's fitness as parents? I sipped my tea and thought for a moment. How ironic that having got rid of me, they then wanted another child but couldn't have one. But why had they suddenly become so desperate for a second child? 'Do you know why, at that precise time,' I asked Aunt Nancy, 'my parents were so keen to have another child?' Aunt Nancy inclined her head, and in a low voice said, 'Well, you see my dear, they wanted a playmate for Ian, didn't they.'

All too soon it was time for me to catch my flight back to Heathrow. I had enjoyed meeting my long-lost Auntie. She seemed a kind soul and very straight up. As I fastened my seatbelt ready for take-off, I mulled over the peculiar story Aunt Nancy had related to me. I felt a mixture of confusion and sadness. Confused because I couldn't understand my father's motives, and sad at the thought of my mother Rose sat pining for another child, pining perhaps for me. Had she longed to try to find me, begged and pestered my father to try to get me back? It was possible. If so, then he may have thought an adoption might be the best way to placate my mother, to shut her up. Or maybe he had genuinely wanted Ian to have a brother or sister. As the plane took off and Glasgow became a tiny speck below us, I thought of Ian, seeing a lonely little boy moved from place to place around the world, perhaps making the odd friend among the children of other servicemen, only to have that friendship severed when one or other of the families got posted.

We seemed to have only just levelled out when the seatbelt signs came on again. As the aircraft began its descent into Heathrow, my mind went into 'what if' mode. What if, for instance, the army had consented to my mother and father's desire to adopt a little playmate for Ian? And what if from day one the two boys had detested one another – would another advertisement have been placed discreetly in the personal column of a provincial newspaper? And what if my parents had become more attached to the new playmate than to Ian? Would he have found himself taken along to a railway station, and there surrendered to complete strangers and an unknown future? Maybe he'd have gone on to become a brickie. Although on second thoughts I can't see that, not with those artistic hands!

Some time after my trip to Glasgow, Ian said he had already told me about Rose and David's plan to adopt a child, on the night of our first meeting. I guess with so much other information tumbling out that evening it just hadn't registered. Apparently as the Christmas of 1955 approached, Rose and David announced to Ian that a little boy would be coming to live with them, and that he was to be Ian's new brother. Then, when Christmas Day arrived, Ian found himself given a double helping of presents. The brother did not arrive. Ian's parents' explained to him that Barnardo's had changed their mind about sending a child, feeling that the army life would be too unstable. Ian now thinks it's possible the army may have intervened with Barnardo's. He was always told the adoption was for his sake, but thinks maybe this was only a fraction of the story. His guess is that our mother was still in torment after the events surrounding my birth and the giving away of me, and that adopting another child was our father's idea. Ian believes it possible our mother was so distressed she *had* actually wanted to come and search for me. Our father therefore arranged a substitute. How disappointed would my mother then have been that Christmas of 1955, when this other promised little boy was snatched away? Even a substitute son would have been something. But, tender as she may have felt towards that child, it would not have been her own. If the adoption plan had been largely down to my father, with her reluctantly agreeing whilst still grieving for me, her emotions must have been on a knife-edge. And what of the Barnardo's boy, presumably selected by our parents as Ian's new brother, looking forward to spending Christmas with his new family, only to be told at the last moment he would not be going. It must have been heart-breaking for the kid.

20

When I had first learned from Ian that our father was dead I had mixed feelings. There was I suppose a slight element of relief at not having to confront him, but only very slight. The opportunity to have met the man who had spawned and spurned me was not one I'd ever have turned down. After all, I'd been searching for him on and off for the whole of my adult life. He was my flesh and blood, and both are thicker than water. To see and hear and touch him would have been fascinating, irresistible, something that had to be done, but it was not to be. I knew that my birth relatives, especially Ian, would fill me in with a lot of information, which should paint a fairly vivid picture of my father. However Ian was able to provide me with something much better.

Back in 1989, perhaps feeling it was time to nail down the past, to capture and preserve something of his ancestry, Ian had set up a conversation with his father. This conversation was conducted in the form of an interview about the old man's life, beginning with his childhood and covering among other things his entry into the military and his experiences in World War II. The stated purpose was to provide a piece of family history, for posterity and first and foremost for the grandchildren. What Ian did not foresee when he began the interview was the reaction which one particular line of questioning was to provoke in our father, and which was to baffle him for some years afterwards.

When Ian told me about this interview I was naturally very interested. But there was one aspect of it that particularly excited me; the whole thing had been recorded on audiotape. Here was the chance to hear my father's voice, a voice from the grave you might say, for the very first time. How would I feel about that? There was only one way to find out. Ian willingly made a copy of the recording for me, which I lost no time taking home. As I inserted the first cassette into the audio system in my living room, I felt a little tingle run down my spine. The tape began running. First came a slight crackle, and something knocking against the microphone. Then, in low, deliberating tones, the voice of my father began to emanate into the room. The accent was distinctively Scottish, not over-broad, but with the slow, authoritative air of someone who thinks carefully as they speak. As in his photograph, I was reminded again of prison officer McKay in *Porridge*, though my father's voice was richer, less nasal. He first announces that the following recording is being made for his grandsons, being Ian's sons, my nephews. He states that he was born in 1917, making him at that time seventy-two years old. He begins to talk of his childhood home, where, despite the poverty, there was great pride in keeping things clean and being personally well turned out. He recalls with pride how his shoes were pointed out by his schoolteacher, as an example to all the class of how well polished shoes should look. His own father he says was a tram driver in Glasgow, who, with a combined war pension and wages, brought in a family income of three pounds and a penny. Ian's voice now comes in on the tape. His tone seems detached, as if he doesn't know his father personally but is carrying out a survey. He asks: 'Would you describe your childhood as happy?' 'Unhappy' is my father's clear response, due chiefly to financial strain and 'many arguments'. He thinks that his mother thought she had married beneath her, and that she may have considered herself intellectually superior to her husband. His mother was, it seems, quite religious, and would read the Bible to her children at home on a Sunday. It was felt she thought her husband seemed 'dull', though 'I don't know'. Ian suggests my father's father may just have been exhausted from working long hours. My father does remember his mother as the dominant one – she ran the house and was if anything 'over-clean'. He recalls again how she regularly cleaned everything in the house, using Brasso and black-leading the stove. I remembered my own mum, Rose Sharp, doing the same at Spring Terrace. Along with the actual black lead, there was always plenty of spirited 'elbow grease' and 'gumption' involved. Cleaning was a virtuous activity in days gone by, no doubt about that, and was one thing that even the poor could take pride in I suppose. Cleanliness was next to godliness, as the saying went. In my father's boyhood home all the children were given chores, which if not completed satisfactorily would earn them a cuff round the ear. 'Were you spanked, smacked?' asks Ian. 'My father would give me six lashes with his belt,' comes the reply, again a punishment usually meted out for not doing the chores. Ian wants to know about the degree of affection that was shown to my father as a child. 'Were you cuddled?' he asks. My father replies that when he was stricken with double pneumonia, then his mother was 'an angel', and would read to him by the bedside, but in general no. Life he concludes was too hard for his parents to be affectionate. One thing he does remember very positively is the food, his mother being an excellent cook and providing nourishing, wholesome meals.

Having been raised as an only child, Ian is naturally curious about sibling relationships, and asks how my father got on with his brothers, and if they ever fought. Yes, says my father, they did fight. 'Could you hold your own?' asks Ian. 'Sometimes – and sometimes you'd get beaten up. That's life.' 'Which sibling were you closest to?' 'Stewart,' confirms my father. 'He was my friend in the family.' Stewart was of course the name he had originally given to me.

There follows a discussion about holidays and recreation.

Though my father did not attend football matches because they couldn't be afforded, I was interested to know that he 'played a lot'. As regards holidays, he says that these were by the sea. 'Do you remember them with affection?' Ian asks. 'Not really,' replies my father. Again, poverty seemed to be what put a damper on everything, and with five members of the family sleeping in one room of a boarding house, going away apparently wasn't much fun. 'Workmen got very little,' he says. 'All the money went to the bosses.'

When Ian asks if there was a strong sense of being Scottish in his childhood community, my father admits he and his contemporaries did then consider themselves superior to the English, whom they thought of as very effete. He didn't actually meet his first Englishman until he joined the army, and at first regarded this man, who was a bugler, as a foreigner. Ian wonders if the fact that he played the bugle confirmed my father's view of the English as effete. My father replies artfully, 'There were some Scotsmen played the bugle too.' At this, Ian seems to give what sounds like a faint chuckle in the background. The shaft of humour seems to lighten the mood after the dour memories of hardship and six of the best. It seemed a good point for me to take a break. I switched off the tape and went into the kitchen for a cup of tea and a biscuit. 'Effete English – how dare he!' I thought, smiling as I took a coaster from the drawer. Ignoring the shortbread, I opened a packet of Bourbons instead. But then, strictly speaking, I was only half-English myself wasn't I? It occurred to me that if Scotland won independence I'd have dual nationality. I couldn't think what the benefits of this would be though, unless they were going to offer us half-Jocks discounted whiskey in exchange for our votes.

I returned to the living room and switched the tape on again. We were back on hard times. My father says there was 'not much joy as a child'. 'What effect,' asks Ian, 'would a joyless childhood have on you – did it make you always want to have fun?' Whatever fun there was for my father apparently did not begin till he joined the army. Here, for the first time he had spending money in his pocket, with wages of ten bob a week being 'a fortune' enabling him to buy a packet of cigarettes a day if he wanted, not just one packet a week. Like my own dad Percy, my father did not he says drink much if at all at this time, and this relative abstinence was common for most soldiers he knew. The drinking started later.

The talk now drifts back to schooldays, where a one-eyed master who had once played in goal for Aberdeen scares young David and his classmates into submission simply by staring at them. The man's missing eye had, apparently, been gouged out by the flailing lace of a football while making a save. I was reminded of English goalie Gordon Banks, who lost his eye not during a match but in a car accident. Next comes a reference to what was perhaps a significant point in my father's early life. Being good at maths and history, and in the top half of the class for these subjects, he passes his eleven-plus with 'flying colours' and is 'third in the whole district'. Following this achievement he is offered a place at the high school. His mother does not allow him to go though because the family cannot afford the additional books and uniform that would be required. The headmaster comments that this is 'a great shame, because David has great potential'. My father adds that he held no grudge against his mother because of this decision. I thought back to my own schooldays. I didn't pass my eleven-plus, with or without flying colours, but nor did thousands of other kids. It didn't seem a big deal.

In 1931 my father's mother developed cancer and died. On her deathbed she gave detailed instructions to my father's sister Grace about the household chores for the morrow. This, knowing she would be gone by the morning. She also outlined plans for how the family should be run during the next ten years. Now there's female practicality for you. She was buried in the family cemetery plot that they had bought. 'You could get six coffins in on top of each other,' says my father. 'It's a lovely old cemetery.' I thought back to Mum's funeral, and how terribly upset I'd been. Had this man felt the same kind of raw pain I'd felt I wondered, or had the harsh Scottish upbringing steeled him to the knowledge that 'in the midst of life we are in death' and these things happen? He had lost his mum younger than I had done mine. After his mother's passing the family 'virtually split up'. Brother Willie was the weaker sibling, and with his mother not around to ensure he had regular good food and warm clothing he succumbed to pneumonia and died.

My father now reminisces on his army career. These memories also trigger his thoughts on politics, which seems quite an emotive subject for him. Coming as he does from both an area and an era of deprivation for working people, my father makes it clear where his allegiances lie. He talks of how wealthy industrialists are so often praised for their hard work. But he is quite scathing about this view, and maintains that if an enterprise is making big profits it can mean only one of two things: either the workers are being paid too little or the goods are overpriced. Listening to my father's voice I got the sense of real conviction. It is the voice of an old Labour man, a firebrand socialist you might say, championing the downtrodden workers against the grasping bosses. But of course, this conversation with my father took place in 1989. The country was still reeling from the 'Thatcher revolution' that had taken on the unions, closed down factories and put skilled workers on the scrap heap. There was also the hated poll tax, which thousands had rebelled against. Emotions did run high at the time, what with the print unions taking on Eddie Shah and the new technology at Wapping and Arthur Scargill and his miners having daily pitched battles with the police. I reflected on how long ago all that seemed now, all those arguments between bosses and workers, the confrontation of 'them and us'. Perhaps everyone simply got tired of fighting. After the long Tory rule of Thatcher and Major, followed by years of New Labour, we have tended to forget how inflamed the political debates used to get. Nowadays we're all supposed to be contented and middle class, despite the fact that the rich are getting richer and the poor poorer. In 1989 my father was obviously still very much a political animal. Perhaps, like old soldiers, ideas never die, they only fade away.

My father then was a working-class man who had lived through the Depression and clearly not forgotten its impact or where he came from. Others though, some of his contemporaries in the army, he is keen to point out, did just the opposite. Eventually my father was promoted from the ranks and became an officer, as did a number of his colleagues. On doing so, he claims, some immediately became conservative, not only in their politics but in their habits and mannerisms. The most serious crime for my father seems to have been the fact that these class traitors changed their accents. He goes on to recount how he once bumped into a man named Archibald, with whom he had formerly been in the ranks. 'Archie,' he called out, but the man ignored him. When my father persisted and reminded his old comrade of their time together as ordinary soldiers, Archibald was apparently forced, grudgingly, to acknowledge him. But what really amazed my father is how Archibald's speech had changed, that his voice had become all posh, like that of an officer born into the upper classes. '"Archie!" I said. "What's wrong with your voice?" – I couldn't believe it!'

There is a pause in the conversation and some coughing, followed by a different sound, a kind of snap, then a fizz. My father is cracking open a can of beer. I'd thought I had heard what sounded like drinking earlier on the tape. The first beers must have been opened right at the start, before the microphone was switched on. My father now says solicitously to Ian, 'Do you want another beer son? Go on …' His voice seems gentler, and there is a sense of the 'kindly man' that Ian has referred to. They could be in a pub together. The interlude is a reminder, that this is a father and son talking. As the beer flows between them I pour myself another cup of tea.

When World War II breaks out my father is sent with the British Expeditionary Force into Europe. As a signals sergeant his responsibility is communications, but with the fighting so 'fluid', trying to run cables is useless. It seems there were no facilities for wireless contact, and semaphore is also ruled out, since any man standing up and waving a flag would soon be shot. The ancient method of signalling with mirrors, the heliograph, is still used by the army. In India they could operate a heliograph over distances up to a hundred and twenty miles. But mirror signalling can only work when the sun is shining, which it rarely did in Belgium during this particular period of the war. My father was therefore made a dispatch rider. On a Norton 500 motorcycle – 'a powerful machine' – he carries messages sometimes for twenty-five miles. Travelling in the pitch-black night with no lights, he often hears the bullets pinging over his head. 'It was exciting, but not very healthy,' he says. One day a corporal asks my father if he will go behind German lines to plead for the return of the corporal's recently captured brother. It was obviously a daft request.

Meeting later the corporal tells him, 'You bastard, you wouldn't go and fetch my brother, and he died.' Well, he could hardly blame my father for that. Sipping my tea in my comfortable living room and gazing out at my neat garden, I wondered: who has the better life – a man who's never been obliged to fight for his country, or one who's done so and lived to tell the tale to his children?

My father has now moved on to the evacuation from Dunkirk. That event as we know, was mayhem, carnage. 'How long were you on the beach?' asks Ian. The answer seems indistinct. 'Some men were selling water,' says my father. Selling it! Apparently, some French blamed the British for the invasion of France, because we'd entered into war with Hitler in 1939. This being the case, during the evacuation from France, British soldiers were sometimes given the wrong directions and sent into the arms of the advancing German forces. 'Some were killed,' he says at one point. I wasn't sure if he meant this for selling the water, but it sounded feasible. 'When you've seen hundreds of men dead,' my father continues, 'ridden over them on your motorbike ... it became meaningless ... a beach carpeted with dead bodies ... horses included. Ian ... I haven't thought about these things for many years ...' As he tails off, Ian comes in with: 'It was a rout?' 'There was no cohesion, it was every man for himself.'

My father's battalion lost 340 men. Having himself been wounded in the leg, he was rescued by boat and taken to a hospital in Liverpool. On the way he witnesses a dramatic incident. A captured young Nazi pilot is offered a cup of tea by a female orderly. The youth impudently flings the scalding liquid back at the woman. Incensed by this insult, half a dozen nearby Brits leap from their sickbeds and set about the German boy, smashing him repeatedly in the face. 'I thought, that's good,' says my father, adding, 'I don't know if he lived or not …' The German arrogance, exemplified by the young pilot, he puts down to the enemy being 'so sure of their victory'. And what about the Brits, I wondered. After the death, horror and humiliation of Dunkirk, how many of our nation believed in their hearts that Britain could still defeat the Nazis? Back home ordinary people were said to have been sharpening anything they could lay their hands on, determined that when the storm troopers did come goose-stepping up the garden path, they'd take one of the bastards with them.

Another beer can sparks open, is poured slowly out. My father clears his throat then picks up his story in the Liverpool hospital following the escape from Dunkirk. His leg has become infected with tetanus and, unbeknown to him at the time, the surgeons are poised to amputate. The leg is saved, though a piece of shrapnel remains inside. Ian asks if the shrapnel gives our father trouble. 'Now and again,' he replies. At the hospital, when the lights go out, some of the nurses get into bed with the patients. There are some further anecdotes, before Ian moves on to the subject of our mother. At what point, he asks our father, did he meet her? My father prevaricates, and Ian repeats the question. Pressed on the matter, my father replies that it must have been 1944. Now comes the unexpected response. He gets quite hot under the collar, hostile almost, and seems to positively resent the question, pointing out that he does not ask Ian about when he and his wife met, the implication being that his son is being intrusive. There is a noise that sounds like a chair scraping back, and after some incoherent mumbling, the tape machine is switched off for the last time. The story of David McEwan's life has come to an abrupt halt, for the time being at least.

Ian was understandably baffled by our father's touchiness over such a simple question. It was only to be some twelve years later, when I came out of the woodwork you might say, and Auntie Margie revealed all, that the reason for that angry reaction became apparent. For the whole of Ian's life till I turned up, the 'official' date that our father and mother first met – in the Biblical sense – must have been given as or assumed to be, at the very earliest, some time after Ernest was killed, 1944. But in fact our parents had met and conceived me in early 1942, while Ernest was risking his life for king and country. But why had my father reacted in such a defensive manner over a matter of dates? Obviously this family secret was still hidden from Ian, but why not just make up a date, or say he couldn't remember exactly? Certainly the question must have caught him off guard. Perhaps it was panic; thinking perhaps that any answer he gave might contradict some other account given long ago and now lost in the fog of time, he had blustered his way out. Possibly he thought my mother might have provided

Ian with her own version of when she met his father. After listening to the tape, it also struck me that our father, on hearing the question about the date, might even have suspected Ian was trying to trap him. That's only speculation of course, but if so it would explain the anger. Inadvertently, Ian had stumbled across a locked closet. Alarmed, our father had leapt to guard the skeleton within from the light of truth, and from the penetrating gaze of his son, a son who might yet condemn him, expose him even. Who knows what fears he may have harboured, as old age and infirmity crept on? I wondered too if there was an element of guilt. Not only the simple guilt at having lied, but at the fact of having cast off a tiny baby, particularly, doing so in such a clinical way. 'Our father's fingerprints all over it,' Ian had commented on the newspaper advertisement. Even a puppy gets 'loving home wanted'. But that baby was his son, his own flesh and blood, and he had called him Stewart after his favourite brother. Who knows, maybe there was a residue of remorse, a faintly glowing ember of sentiment that had survived beneath the hard soldier's no-nonsense practicality and down the long passage of the years. Perhaps the guilt, if any, lay more in what he'd put my mother through by forcing her to give away her child. If my father had ever felt any regret or sorrow over me, it must have been buried very deeply. Like his other memento from the war, the once-sharp shard of shrapnel, invisible yet lodged permanently within him, had I also given him an occasional twinge of discomfort? 'Does it bother you?' 'Now and again ...'

21

With the invaluable help of the Salvation Army, I had traced my biological parents and found my relatives. And with my 'new' family's assistance I now knew a considerable amount about both Rose and David, the two people who brought me, their first child together, into this world and with whom I will always be connected. But there was still an unanswered question: exactly why did they dispose of that first child? Apart from the fact that Rose was married to Ernest at that time and I was illegitimate – admittedly very significant in 1942 – there had to be another reason for the uniquely swift and uncompromising way I was got rid of. If Rose had wanted to keep her newborn – and it's hard to believe a mother's instincts wouldn't dictate strongly in that direction – could a compromise not have been reached? If my mother Rose had fallen out of love with Ernest, or never been close to him, and my father was more to her than a brief encounter, then surely they could have 'worked something out'. There had to be another factor involved, but what was it? The answer, when it came, was from an unexpected source.

There has never been any doubt in my mind that had I been conceived in a later era, my mother, having found herself pregnant, would have taken herself, or more likely been ordered by my father to the nearest clinic and I would have disappeared in a puff of smoke up an incinerator chimney, my life over before it began. But in 1942 circumstances were considerably different for a woman finding herself 'in trouble'. Apart from the legal and health risks of the back-street abortionist, the options were, to say the very least, restricted. Most likely would be a prolonged stay with a distant relative until the little bastard was born, before being either adopted or bunged in a kids' home. My parents decided on what some would say was a truly unique approach to their 'little inconvenience'.

But I wondered who decided what? As I say, from what Ian told me I had the feeling my mother and father didn't sit down over dinner and have a friendly heart to heart about what was best for everyone. More likely, as soon as he heard about the pregnancy, my father, with all the sensitivity befitting an NCO from the tough side of Glasgow, would have ordered his mistress to get shot of it. Remembering Ian's remark that the advert in the *Reading Mercury* bore our father's imprint made me think he had also conformed to the stereotype of the tight-fisted jock. Adding the word 'loving' before 'home wanted for baby boy' would surely have cost extra. Money might not buy love, but ignoring love can save you money.

As I turned the question of 'why?' over in my mind, I recalled another wartime anecdote that our father had related to Ian. It is an amusing but also slightly unsettling story, the first half of which occurs during the war, while the British Expeditionary Force in Europe is on the back foot. The Germans are advancing and our father's company comes under fire. Among the casualties, he sees a comrade by the name of Latimer get shot in the neck. With blood spurting from his throat it is clear to everyone the man is a goner. Our father and his comrades wrap Latimer in the 'death blanket' that every soldier carries, and leave him in the field. Years later in 1953, my father is in Woking, Surrey, attending the funeral of another old soldier. It is a full regimental affair, and a band has come down from Scotland for the occasion. As the musicians arrive and set up, my father stares in amazement. For who should be the sergeant of this band? It is none other than Latimer, the man my father and his comrades had left for dead on the battlefield some fourteen years ago. 'Latimer!' he exclaims incredulously. 'What are you doing here?' Latimer's response is unclear, though one can imagine he might have mixed feelings himself at the unexpected reunion. 'We thought you were dead,' says our father. 'We saw blood pouring from your throat.' It transpired that the advancing Germans had patched Latimer up and that he'd been taken as a prisoner of war. 'We felt,' says our father on the tape recording, 'that he had cheated death.' Now, just suppose that in 1953 aged eleven, I had tracked down my father and turned up at Woking on that same day. 'Hello Dad, how's it going, remember me? I'm David, the one you got rid of. You named me Stewart though, after Uncle Stewart. How's Mum by the way? Tell her thanks for the birthday card. I hear I've got a little brother now. Ian isn't it? How old would he be, about four or five by now ...' First Latimer rising from the grave like Lazarus in front of my father, then me appearing out of thin air, and at a funeral. I think seeing two ghosts in one day would have been too much, even for my father's grizzled Glaswegian upper lip. He'd have either hit the deck or, like his old pal Archibald, the one who'd become a toff, had done, tried to give me the cold shoulder and deny all knowledge of me. Judging by the way he'd clammed up about when he and my mother first met it seems likely he'd have had me frogmarched off the premises. I think I'd have put up a bloody good fight first though.

Just suppose I had met both my biological parents, when both of them were still in good health. What would they have made of me, or me of them? How do you introduce yourself to a guy who fathered you nearly sixty years ago; what's the etiquette in such situations? Debrett's has no answer. Again, would I simply walk in and say, 'Hello Daddy, I'm the product of your adultery', or give him a good slap and tell him not to do it again? As he'd have been an old man the latter would probably be unnecessary and inappropriate. My brothers are divided on what his reaction to my sudden appearance may have been. Roy thinks that even with modern nailed-on DNA evidence my father would have denied everything to his dying day. Ian on the other hand thinks he would have wanted to shake hands, go to the nearest pub and get pissed. The reality would probably have been somewhere in the middle. He may even have come round to accepting me as his son, maybe sending a birthday card once in a while. As for my mother, after she'd got over the embarrassment and shame of giving me away to complete strangers at a month old, would she too have accepted me? Or would the intervening years have been too great a gap? Now I'll never know.

If I had met my father, I would certainly have asked him that question 'Why did you get rid of me?' Ian's view was that that the decision to offload me was largely down to our father. OK. But did anyone else share this view? I could readily believe Ian's assessment and had no reason to doubt my brother, who after all had been brought up by the man. But should I make my mind up about my father solely on this basis? I wanted to find out for myself, shed more light on the matter, and wondered if I should conduct my own investigations to get another angle on the man who had made me, and what had made him tick. But how would I go about it? Perhaps I should try to track down someone else who had known David McEwan independently of the family. If it was my father who had decreed I should be parted forever from my mother, I had to know why.

Quite out of the blue, what I was looking for fell into my lap, or more precisely, into Ian's. In February 2007, shortly after the story of Ian and me being brothers appeared in the papers, Ian received a letter. It was from, of all people, a man who had served with my father in the army, a man by the name of John Shotton. He had seen the press coverage of our story. The dates in question were from 1962 to 1965, the location 7, Armoured Workshops, Fallingbostel, BAOR (British Army on The Rhine).

'Your father,' wrote Mr Shotton (to Ian), 'was the Adjutant there ... and I got to know David McEwan very well. Of my many duties one was to take the REME ski side down to the Alps to train then compete in the BAOR and UK championships.' He recalls that in 1963–64 he 'went down in mid December before the team and was accompanied by a young teenager ... travelling all day and ending late in the pitch black of night ... descending and looking down from about three hundred feet at a village lit by the lights on Christmas trees. It was magical. I wonder if that is how you remembered it, for the teenager was you, being David's son. David had asked me to take you. At Fallingbostel ... no one had so much as a clue about the truth of things, so I write to let you know how I remembered your father and mother ...' The 'truth of things' I took to mean the events in my father's private life in 1942 concerning me, and his own subsequent memories of my father and mother.

'In my time in the army, of the ninety or so officers I served with there would be no more than half a dozen I'd have gone out of my way to meet again and at the top of that list would be David McEwan.' Hearing this I was tempted to wonder what the others must have been like. But let the jury remain out. I couldn't let my own feelings obscure the picture of my father that I was trying to see. I read on. On my father's physical appearance, Mr Shotton was also complimentary: '... carried himself very well indeed, good looking ... his uniform immaculate ... in all things exemplary, a natural leader.' Later he maintains that David McEwan was 'an absolute delight to talk to, not least because of his high IQ ... I trusted him absolutely. He I'm sure wouldn't talk about me behind my back ... I know for sure others did ... nor did he ever have anything adverse to say to me about others nor I to him ...' It was clear that my father and Mr Shotton had got on well, and he was clearly speaking from his honest memory of the time. The most interesting part though, certainly for me, was yet to come.

'Some reflections,' wrote Mr Shotton, 'from a soldier's point of view on what was said in the *Sunday Times* of 21 January 2007: whether married or unmarried, a soldier's first duty is to the army ... when the call is made it is to be obeyed the family and/or private life comes second. I've seen warrant officers reduced to the ranks for being unfit for duty (too much drinking), officers cashiered for adultery.' I read this last sentence again. Now we were getting to the heart of the matter. 'The giving away of the month-old baby and the advert for it in the paper I guess was all your father's doing, and it was as tragic as it was unavoidable.' Unavoidable? Well, that's debatable, I thought.

'Had the husband found out about it he would of course have been incensed about it, but so would the army, and your father's army career would have been finished then and there — or at best would have gone on his records and finished him later ... the instigation and wording of the advert is entirely your father's: "complete surrender" is exactly the sort of phrase he used, the clarity and uncompromising nature ... has your father's stamp.' This observation closely echoed Ian's first remarks to me on the subject. It's a wise man knows his own father they say. 'Your mother,' maintained Mr Shotton, 'had no choice in the matter. It was either this or ruination and destitution with three children, if her husband were to respond as she thought he would.' No choice. Here the echo was of Auntie Margie, and her memory of my mother chanting 'I had to, I just had to' over and over as the train and destiny dragged her remorselessly from her infant child, now in the arms of strangers. It was the severing of a tie that was destined to remain un-joined for more than half a century, by which time that young mother on the train would be an old woman, quite unaware that the pleasant stranger who one day appeared with tulips was her little boy whom she had once cuddled and rocked gently to sleep.

The written testimony in a seemingly candid letter from an old comrade seemed to amply support Ian's verdict on my father's leading role in Operation Complete Surrender. As for the motive, Mr Shotton had more to say about the crucial matter of my father's career. "The adoption would keep your father clean with the army. The army will not tolerate adultery: clearly it has to maintain discipline and morale ... at home and overseas ... I've no doubt that with "active service" involved, one would have seen the service at its most ruthless ... I saw a major cashiered for such an offence, an offence incidentally for all ranks ... If in 1942 the army had discharged him on account of the affair, he would have had no one to turn to, no work to go to. No qualifications meant no future, and he knew it. The army was all he had. A terrible thing though it was ... it seems adoption was the best for all concerned including the baby, for it was the lesser of two evils ...' Well, that was nice to know.

But at least I had my answer. My father surrendered me, his first-born son, for his career. I thank you Mr Shotton.

22

Ian has been dubbed the 'supreme novelist of his generation', a high-profile author whose books sell hundreds of thousands of copies internationally, winning him coveted prizes and public honours. Ian's novels have been enjoyed by millions of people and their contents discussed enthusiastically by readers, book clubs, TV panellists, university professors and academics all over the world. I am a locally known bricklayer and jobbing builder. Such contrasts are what the media seemed to like most about the story of Ian and me, the polar opposites of our lifestyles and chiefly the fact that the Ian who turned out to be my brother was 'the' Ian McEwan, the celebrated author. Nobody in Ian's profession had heard of me before of course, but I decided that having already started writing my life story, I'd follow my brother's suggestion and carry on with it. In the early stages of putting this book together, some of those who looked at the manuscript suggested it might be better if it were written more in my 'own voice'. As it happened, these people had never met me when they saw the manuscript. How did they know what my 'own voice' sounded like? I believe they did however know I was a bricklayer who had left school at fifteen and received no formal academic education since. Could no one think outside the blocks? If I was expected to write like a bricklayer, how do bricklayers write? I'd heard of chick-lit; perhaps there was something called 'brick-lit' too.

For my part, there were things I didn't 'get' about Ian's world, such as some of the discussions among his colleagues. I've seen an article where he describes a letter of reply he'd just composed to a harsh critic, which he was intending to send to the *Spectator*. Over a lunch, he shows this letter to some literary pals, who look embarrassed. 'There's a dangler in that first line,' one of them whispers to him. Ian has begun the letter 'Sir' not 'Dear Sir' and now he seems to realise this sounds pompous. At least, I think that's the gist of it. But I'm still a bit mystified – I mean, dangler, what's that all about? I read an interview with Martin Amis – an author with whom Ian is often ranked – in which he said something to the effect that a person couldn't just walk off the assembly line and become an author. I wonder why not – something to do with the danglers perhaps? Mind you, it's easy to take the mickey out of things you don't understand, and to be fair, if Ian walked in on a building site conversation the scaffolding might not be the only thing going over his head.

I'd never come across any of Ian's books before we met, but I've read all of them now. Some, I have to say, I enjoyed more than others. After Ian's publishers sent me a parcel of his collected works, I joked with him about how the postman had eyed me curiously as I signed for the plain brown box, and how he was still giving me funny looks – i.e. did he suspect I was buying 'adult material' from Denmark – nudge, nudge. When I mentioned this Ian was kind enough to indulge the adolescent humour in me. Maybe he shared a streak of it himself. If in fact we did both have a weakness for schoolboy humour, would that be down to genetics? Scientists are gradually identifying genes for everything else from infertility to obesity, so who knows? Ian can discuss complex subjects like genetics and humanism – of which he seems a great advocate. He has also written some very macabre stories. However he is not above fooling around, in fiction or in life. I can confirm that socially he's actually quite jovial and good company. The darkness, as far I can tell, is all in his books. If you want to find a tortured soul, perhaps look inside a comedian. As regards foolery in his work, Ian describes in one novel a particular psychological condition – named after a Dr Clerambault and also known as 'erotomania' – from which one of his characters suffers. He gives details of the symptoms and the clinical terminology and includes in an appendix a psychiatric paper written by Clerambault. Though the condition and its originator are real, Ian made up the psychiatric paper. It did however convince many experts when the book was first published.

Piltdown Man and the spaghetti trees all over again. What would be similar behaviour in my line of work? Well I have called myself a 'brickologist' when stating my occupation, either that or 'an artist in burnt clay'. On each occasion whomever I was speaking to has looked very earnest and interested, unless and until they realised I was pulling their leg. Well, builders tend to get a bad press, don't they? Nowadays though I love all these reality TV programmes about cowboys who take money up front only to bodge the job and do a runner, sometimes leaving the client's property in a worse state than before. The day after one of these shows is broadcast my phone usually starts ringing with offers of work. I always make a point of never asking for any money in advance, not even for materials. Most of my customers are of the generation that don't expect to pay unless they are satisfied, but also take pride in settling their bills on time. As long as I do a good job for people I have no worries about bad debts. This might sound like an advertisement but I honestly don't need one. Occasionally people have told me 'how marvellous it must be to be a bricklayer'. I agree and then ask if they would be pleased for their daughter to marry one. The response is often, shall we say, hesitant. Don't they know brickies' wives are the new wags? It said so in the *Daily Telegraph*, so it must be true.

So, Ian and I have both, in different ways, been known to gently pull the wool over people's eyes. Maybe when the Human Genome Project is complete they'll have identified the DNA that makes someone prone to 'winding others up'.

In a TV documentary Oliver Reed's brother once revealed how he and Ollie decided early on that the best way to ensure continuing publicity was a bit of 'bad boy' behaviour. Thus piss-ups and punch-ups became Reed's stock-in-trade and helped maintain his box-office status. Nowadays being uncouth and getting arrested are par for the course for Pete Doherty and his ilk. Virtue is its own reward but vice grabs the headlines and sells records, films and T-shirts by the skip-load. When the story of our meeting first hit the headlines I'm sure Ian and I could have cooked up some juicy scandal about how we hated each other, but the shocking truth is that we got on quite well and, touch wood, still do. There's one thing Ian has lived with for many years and that is the scrutiny of the media. They say there's no such thing as bad publicity. Is that really true? Ask the person on the receiving end. Some people assume that being in the news whatever is always important for an author, and that, as Oscar Wilde said, 'There's only one thing worse than being talked about – and that's *not* being talked about'. Not everyone agrees. Ian maintains that scrutiny of his personal life does not help his books, and gets in the way of writing. We live in a different world to that of Wilde, in some ways more tolerant, but in others more vicious. The modern media machine takes no prisoners. It can be a fickle beast, a double-edged sword and in some cases, a downright two-faced bastard. Dr Johnson, taking the 'all publicity is good' idea a step further said that 'fame is a shuttlecock; it has to be hit from both ends of the room to stay in the air'. There seems an element of truth in that. Nobody can, and probably shouldn't try to, please all of the people all of the time.

Ian has had a lot of good, well-deserved press where it is relevant, i.e. concerning his work. However, the nearer you get to the apex of your chosen career, the greater the likelihood of a green-eyed monster called jealousy, lurking around the corner ready to kick you in the nuts at the first opportunity. When the plagiarism charges were flung against Ian, a number of his fellow authors were also quick to come to his defence. Some critics then claimed this support had all been organised by his publishers, that they'd closed ranks, were all cronies sticking together. You can't win sometimes, can you? It's not a problem I've been faced with so far. I'm a brickie, not a novelist, so plagiarism doesn't enter my world, and my walls frequently resemble walls built by other brickies. Intellectual property rights don't yet extend to bricklaying.

My own direct experience with the media only began in January 2007. When news of my connection with Ian broke, I simply could not believe the scale of interest. In retrospect, I did not realise how the media would take up my story, and the consequences that would follow from an initial interview with a provincial newspaper. Was this to be my Pandora's Box? Within a few days of my approaching my local paper, the *Oxford Mail*, the story got picked up and went national, then global. Pictures of Ian and me jumped out of the pages of almost every 'serious' newspaper, and a few of the tabloids too. My phone began ringing the same morning, and went on ringing. Journalists offered increasingly large sums of money for further photos and interviews. Two newshounds who'd been phoning separately turned out to be working for the same paper, and had been trying to outbid one another for an interview with me. I had phone calls from very excited-sounding people in America, again wanting interviews, again offering money. I turned all offers down, following Ian's advice to 'keep your powder dry'. By the third day of this activity I was feeling decidedly uncommunicative, and was sitting indoors in the morning with a cup of tea and the phone's ring-tone switched off, determined not to answer it. I had my front room blinds in the half-closed position, just enough for me to look out to the road, without allowing anyone to see in. I was just starting to relax when I saw a taxi pull up outside, not an everyday sight in our quiet street. Out stepped a smartly dressed young woman who marched promptly up to my front door and rang the bell. She was from some glossy American magazine, which judging by the copy she handed me was a sort of US version of *Hello*. Goodbye, I politely told her, for now anyway. How had she got my address? She hadn't been the first reporter to come to my home. Journalists also managed to find the addresses of my half-siblings and doorstep them for a 'comment', an intrusion that they found very unwelcome, and I very much regret occurring.

The lady from the *Oxford Mail* did a very courteous and professional job with the original story. By the time it had filtered out to the nationals, though, a certain amount of padding was creeping in, some of it a bit speculative. In one review section I was described as 'a large florid man of action'. If twelve-and-a-half stone is large, then so be it. As for florid, the description can only have been based on the photo of Ian and myself seen in the *Oxford Mail*. At the time I'd been using some evil prescribed cream called Efudix on my face. This is a legacy of spending some fifty summers outside in the building industry, with the inevitable skin cancer problems. This is a vicious type of cream that burns the affected cells, leaving the face temporarily 'florid'. And as regards 'man of action', was that a journalist's stereotyped assumption that builders can get a bit physical on occasion?

Nature or nurture, which matters most in the forming of a person? Peter Cook was once asked very seriously what his recent comedy film, which involved pirates, was all about. He replied, in equally serious tones, that the film 'examined whether piracy was environmental or hereditary'. To find out what makes a novelist or a bricklayer, where would you start? In Ian's case, probably natural ability combined with the things he collided with in his youth – aspects of his schooling, the books he came across that made him fascinated with the English language and story-telling. And why did I become a brickie? You could include a love of being out in the open, working with my hands (I originally wanted to be a chippy remember) and maybe chance in the shape of Leonard Walden, the man who never looked at me when he took me on as a bricklaying apprentice. To go further back, and speculate about what I might be doing today if my parents David and Rose McEwan had brought me up, is an interesting exercise. But it's not one you can draw any definite conclusions from, except to say I'd be different in some respects, as, probably, would Ian. I'd perhaps have gone into a white-collar job rather than a blue collar one, but more than that, who knows?

If nature unaided has any influence on personality, then Ian and I will find we are alike. The temptation is to look for similarities that aren't there, and to find them. As for nurture, I had a warm and loving upbringing. Ian's childhood seems, in certain reports, to have been colder. His mother was intimidated by our father, whom Ian describes as 'kindly' though always frustrated and restless, as well as sometimes drunken and occasionally violent. But 'he loved me fiercely', says Ian. The fierce love of a military man for his son, an artistic child, can sometimes be painfully hard to convey, and to reciprocate. But without such challenges in his early life, would Ian have become the hugely successful author he is today? The grit in the oyster that produces the pearl is an old cliché. Maybe in Ian's case it's true. One of Ian's favourite poets is Philip Larkin, who believed that most people are basically unhappy. Larkin also famously wrote, 'They fuck you up your mum and dad.' Mine tucked me up. Ian says that during his childhood he was mostly just fed and monitored. Being often lonely at school he was 'always on the lookout for the one true best friend'. If Rose and David McEwan had kept me, and Ian and I had grown up together as brothers, would we have fought jealously with one another, been a regular Cain and Abel? Or would I have been that one true best friend to him? Many siblings have that good fortune.

Ian was an only child and so was I. As far back as 1982, my brother wrote a long and detailed article in which he talks about his particular experience of growing up without brothers or sisters. It is a moving piece, and many of his memories of a childhood without siblings are like my own, positive ones. He ponders a stereotypical image of the 'only child', suggesting the words conjure up a picture of 'a doleful eight-year-old; nose pressed against a window pane watching a sunlit procession of merry children, siblings all, chanting and cart-wheeling past his house'. I can't say I was ever a 'doleful' child at any age. Most of the time I would more likely have been one of the noisy kids outside, though kicking a football, and with mates rather than siblings obviously. As he gathered opinions on the subject, one friend of Ian (who was from a large family) confessed to him that when growing up she had thought the term 'only child' was in fact 'lonely child'. Ian asked other friends what words best described only children they had known. Several came back with things like: selfish, self-absorbed, spoiled, over-ambitious and demanding. Of course, people *with* siblings never have these traits, do they? Hmm. Only children, clearly, have 'an image problem'. Ian, on behalf of only children everywhere, offered his own suggested list of their qualities. He included: being sensitive as well as secure, being well equipped to give and take love, having a deep sense of responsibility and possessing a rich imagination. Whether Ian felt inclined to revise this list after he had met me, I cannot say! (The curious thing I suppose is that we're both now, sort of, no longer only children, or perhaps that should be, no longer 'only adults'.) The most important trait of only children, Ian reckoned, was that they were not afraid of solitude, that they even enjoyed it. He says: 'I know of people who grew up in large families who cannot keep their own company for more than an hour or two, after which they begin to wonder if they exist.' In my own case, whilst I enjoy socialising, I certainly don't mind my own company. In fact lately I've more often than not worked alone, the solitude balanced pleasantly by the occasional chat over a cup of tea with my customer.

In the 1982 article Ian also expresses some very poignant recollections, especially when describing the time his newly adopted brother was due to arrive. 'After I was born, my mother was not able to have any more children, and when I was seven, my parents decided to adopt a little boy to keep me company.' He describes how 'elaborate arrangements' were made to welcome Bernard (he even knew his name), who would be joining the family in time for Christmas. Our mother baked delicious mince pies and Ian helped our father tie bunches of balloons around the house, including in 'our' bedroom – the room he was all set to share with Bernard. Appropriate Christmas presents had been thoughtfully chosen, caringly wrapped and put out for Bernard. 'I doubt,' says Ian, 'if ever a more loving, expectant household stood ready to greet an adopted child.' Ian not only knew the name of his brother-to-be, he knew what he looked like, or at least, he had been told Bernard had fair hair. As a sensitive, artistic child, Ian would naturally have built up a strong picture in his imagination of the companion with whom he would soon be sharing his life so intimately. Surely he would have been equally if not more excited than our parents were about this impending miracle which was going to happen to him. As the arrival of his brother drew nearer, he began, he says, 'to address him in my mind'. Picturing this scene in the McEwan household, one can feel all the warmth and wonder of Christmas – mother lovingly turning out mince pies in the kitchen, father and young son hanging balloons, the aroma of the pine tree beautifully trimmed and sparkling with tinsel and burnished holly, the prettily displayed presents. Ian must have felt as keenly as any other little boy the special sense of magic and enchantment that fills the air at Christmas time. But for the McEwans this was no ordinary Christmas. This year a visitor far more magical than Santa Claus was coming to their home. Ian's new brother would henceforward be part of the family, and for Ian it must have seemed that a new phase of his own life was about to begin. In his imaginary conversations with Bernard he would probably have also been envisaging all manner of exciting activities the two of them could share in the weeks and months and years that lay ahead.

Ian would not have been the only one counting the days till Bernard's arrival. For our mother, the occasion must have been highly charged, her heart brimming with expectation. The message of Christmas is one of healing love, a celebration of the birth of a child who was destined to change the world, turning darkness to light, despair to hope, sin to glorious salvation. For my mother, her years of painful yearning, of longing to somehow set right or make up for the clandestine act she had committed on that windswept station in the desperate days of the war, were about to end. That Christmas, having taken the decision to adopt, it must have felt to my mother like a kind of redemption was due, a new dimension to her life that would in some way repair the past, and help to restore her peace of mind. Was it any coincidence that the child she and my father had chosen was, like me, a fair-haired boy? Then, at the last moment, she was told she could not have the boy after all. My mother must have been devastated. It seems though that intense disappointment was not her only emotion. Ian says that both parents, our mother especially, were deeply stung by the 'insinuation' behind the rejection. Although the ostensible reason given was the unsuitability of itinerant army life for a child (though presumably the Barnardo's people had known our father's military position all along, so why was it made an issue at such a late stage?), there is the sense that my mother's pride was hurt, the feeling that she and my father had failed some kind of test, that they were judged not good enough. The episode seems such a painful one for all those involved, my mother, father and Ian. But also, even especially, for Bernard, who presumably had been told that at Christmas he would have a new home, a proper one with a family and presents to boot. Imagine the scene when some official broke the news to him that he wouldn't be going after all. It brings a lump to the throat even to think about it. And was it the right decision, or was it horribly misjudged? Who's to say Bernard wouldn't have thrived on a life on the move, seeing different countries, and of course, having Ian for a brother? Perhaps, as Ian says, the army for some reason intervened. If one day we hear from Bernard, or others involved, we may have a clearer picture. Till then, all we can be sure of is that in this sad Christmas story, it wasn't a case of no room at the inn, but the wise men decreeing that the one on offer wasn't good enough.

As far as the seven-year-old Ian was concerned, having already got to know Bernard in his thoughts, the adoptive brother remained, he says, 'real enough' – he had seen Bernard's Christmas presents, 'there were his things' – and he 'adopted him as an invisible playmate'. The fact Ian created this brother in his imagination might suggest something lacking in his childhood. Psychologists might call it compensation. On the other hand, the fact that he didn't let mere circumstances spoil what he'd so looked forward to could equally be regarded as a triumph of mind over matter. From one perspective, with the brother already alive in his imagination, it meant he could remain perfect, or unaltered, just as Ian had invented him.

I wonder how I would have compared at that time, to the friend who lived so vividly in Ian's imagination. Supposing I had come back, and we had grown up together? Would there have been an instant bond, the two of us becoming permanent close companions? Or would I have seemed to Ian a bit of a country ruffian, a sort of William Brown to his Jennings? Most likely we'd have been a bit chalk and cheese at first, him bookish, me more practical, but perhaps that could have been the basis of a very good friendship. As far as books were concerned I could maybe have matched him on Cervantes, having learned about Don Quixote from two consecutive teachers. From there on, who knows? We might have jointly perused Poe or had a dip into Dickens, or if too hot for book learning, maybe climbed the wall of that big house together for an illicit dip in that lovely swimming pool. Well, we do already share a gene pool! Our brotherhood is just beginning, and the unusual thing about it is that our parents are not around to make it, or fuck it up. So from here on I guess it's a case of us watching this space, the lifetime of it that lies between us, and seeing if it narrows.

23

Nobody has elocution lessons any more. Unless it's to knock the plum out of their mouth and give them the common touch, teach 'em to speak estuary English or mockney like. Public figures from Tony Blair to Jamie Oliver have been accused of putting it on, deliberately downplaying a middle- or upper-class background in order to win votes or favour, and now Old Etonian David Cameron's dropping his aitches along with his tie. Some of these accusations can be unfair though. In the case of Jamie Oliver, people who remember him from the days he cooked in a pub, and they should know, swear he's for real. My brother Ian freely admits he changed the way he spoke. As a child he expressed himself like our mother Rose, as he points out in his article 'Mother Tongue':

'It's a lot of cars today id'n it?' she would say. Or: 'Look at them cows … and that black one, he looks daft dud'n he?'

These remarks were in fact made while Ian was taking his mother out for a drive in the country in 1994. 'Yes, he does,' replies Ian about the cow. It's a long time since he spoke like Rose. How, and why, did he change? The 'how' happened partly by itself, through being a youthful bookworm and partly by conscious effort. By reading novels by Graham Greene and Iris Murdoch among others, he gradually picked up on the correct pronunciation, and stopped saying things like 'skelington' 'cestificate' and 'chimley'. He says he also got rid of double negatives – so presumably the 'skelington' could no longer sing 'I ain't got no body ...'

When asked how my brother and I differed, one thing I mentioned was our voices. Ian speaks the Queen's English, the way some would say it should be spoken. My voice on the other hand lends itself more to that of an Oxfordshire hillbilly, and always has done. Why was it Ian's accent changed and mine didn't? The obvious answer is our differing influences. Just as an Englishman who's lived for years in America might end up talking like JR, so the circles Ian moved in altered his voice. Long prior to that, our respective primary schools were apparently little different, so then we may have sounded far more alike than we do now. And from age eleven to sixteen there also seems to have been comparatively little divergence between us; my secondary school was fairly bog-standard, and Ian's, though a boarding school, was also a state institution, and in his words 'not posh', with most of the other boys being Londoners from working-class backgrounds. So who knows, maybe Ian had a bit of a cockney phase, though if there's any trace of it left, or the childhood burr, it would take a Professor Higgins to spot it. And since the social circles I move in today are largely the same ones I inhabited in my boyhood, the Oxfordshire hillbilly has stayed put, with I suspect, not many layers for Professor Higgins to peel back.

Our mother also changed the way she spoke, but unlike Ian, this wasn't a permanent change; rather it was something she dipped in and out of according to who (or whom) she was conversing with. It's debatable how class-divided the British Army is today, but in the 1950s it was almost certainly more so. Men like my father could rise through the ranks, but as Ian says, they rarely got promoted higher than major. The great divide, in the military and in British society generally, was marked by the way you spoke. Ian remembers in the mid 1950s taking a train ride with our mother when a 'lady' entered the carriage. As she and Rose got talking, Ian noticed our mother's voice alter as she tried to speak 'correctly' like the lady. Years later he heard her do the same thing when talking to the colonel's wife during a regimental function. Why did she do this? It would be easy to think her foolish or pretentious, but people did worry much more about being thought 'common' in those days. Nowadays everyone's urged to 'be yourself'. In my mother's day, particularly in social situations, this must have been easier said than done. She obviously felt she had to speak nicely among nice people. And surely it's just good manners to try to speak the language of your host, or someone you meet on a train.

Remembering our father's attitude to his comrades who changed their accents begs the question of what he thought of his wife doing so, albeit only when the situation demanded. He was perhaps luckier in that a Scottish accent has always in a way been able to stand on its own two feet, is more authoritative in its own right. If he had been brought up speaking with the same country burr as my mother, maybe he too would have modified it. With my mother, the 'nice' voice seems to have been just an accoutrement, like a smart dress put on for a formal occasion. She'd always be relieved to slip into something more comfortable again though. In 1970 my mother was admitted to hospital in London for a stomach operation. Being a military hospital, even the women were separated according to their husbands' ranks, and she'd been placed in a ward with other officers' wives. However, as soon as she was able, she'd apparently lost no time visiting the other wards, where she'd palled up with the wives of privates and corporals. Despite my father's elevation, these were obviously still 'her' people, and Ian recalls that when he went to collect his mother, the girls were saying an emotional farewell to the woman they all said had lent them such a sympathetic ear during their stay in hospital. My mother, then, did retain her own identity as far as both her speech and sense of belonging were concerned. Her son Ian on the other hand left his native voice behind more or less for good.

As he was growing up, Ian knew that our father's drunkenness upset our mother, though she never dared challenge him. During his years at boarding school he didn't intervene, being he says, like our mother, 'too tongue-tied' in the face of our father's 'iron certainties'. He began holidaying abroad with friends in his mid teens and after that 'drifted away' and 'saved my darker thoughts for my fiction where fathers, especially the one in *The Cement Garden,* were not kindly presented'. By the time he'd reached his twenties however, Ian says he was often in the position of defending or trying to defend Rose against David, or 'promote her cause somehow', and made what efforts he could to speak up for her. One serious argument occurred when he visited our parents in Germany. Our mother had been offered a part-time job running a mobile library in the barracks. Our father, presumably being an old-fashioned chauvinist who thought this would reflect badly on him, refused to allow her to work. Ian took our mother's side but the old man wouldn't budge. Two years later though, when the library opportunity came up again, he did concede, so maybe Ian's influence did play some part. I wonder if the fact that it had been a library job had touched some additional nerve in our father. Bearing in mind his own father had considered himself less educated than his wife, perhaps our father had felt the same kind of relative inferiority, despite, or because of, what Ian describes as his 'ferocious intelligence'.

With the 1970s of course came women's lib, and a lot of publicity about how many wives were still treated as just goods and chattels by their husbands. Ian read Germaine

Greer's book *The Female Eunuch* when it came out, and thought it was 'a revelation'. He resolved that the female characters in his books would now be 'the repository of all the goodness that men fell short of' and that 'pen in hand' he was 'going to set my mother free'. What he actually used was a typewriter, given to him as a birthday present from our father. 'At home, there was violence in the air. There always had been, but only now could I really see it for what it was, and begin to judge it. My father, I know, felt he had a right to it, and it was no one's business but his own. When I was visiting my parents in the late 1970s, Rose told me the latest. I was inclined to believe her and offered to talk to David. The idea horrified her. It would make things worse when I left.' The first thing Ian wrote on the typewriter given to him by his father was a letter back to the old man, saying that though he loved him, hitting our mother was a criminal act, and that if necessary he would come out from England and see both the military police and his father's commanding officer. He gave the letter to our mother, who, too scared to even have it in the house, promptly destroyed it. After this, according to Ian, 'Matters went on much as before, and what settled the problem in the end was only mellowing age, illness and growing dependency.' Distressing as these incidents were, Ian is also understandably concerned to present our father fairly. In a letter to me he stressed that the facts as he remembers them should be kept in perspective: 'Our father was no angel, but I would hate to see him falsely characterised as a habitual wife beater. There were some bad episodes in the early 1950s (witnessed not by me but by a relative). Then there was a recurrence in the late 1970s in Germany, again not witnessed by me but described to me by our mother. That's when I wrote that letter. Certainly, in these later instances, "beat" would be too strong a word. In all those years I never saw any violence.' For the vast majority of the time, says Ian, our father adored our mother. And he was, as far as Ian knows, faithful to her.

Leaving my father's situation aside, in how many households has domestic violence at some level cast its shadow, and in how many does it still do so? Whether every night or once in a blue moon, what makes a man use violence on a woman, inflicting fear and suffering on the person he supposedly loves? Some say it's to do with inadequacy or with childhood – that if you were physically abused in your home, you will pass on that abuse to others. 'Man hands on misery to man', to quote Philip Larkin again. I don't know if the family background argument is true, or if it's a convenient excuse for some people. What I have learned is that in my father's hometown of Govan, he is remembered as a fine upstanding fellow, something of a hero. Domestic violence of whatever degree, has always, by definition I suppose, been something that goes on behind closed doors. There are still men who think that it's par for the course to keep your woman in check with the occasional right-hander. Only a few years ago a very well known and otherwise well respected actor publicly said more or less this. He is also Scottish incidentally.

If my mother resented my father's drunken and occasionally violent behaviour, it did not stop her caring for him throughout his final illness, until in fact he died in her arms. She obviously saw it as the most natural thing to do. It is very hard to see into the most private relationship of all, another person's marriage. The interdependence of two people can weather a lot of storms. Unspoken compromises and sacrifices are made all the time, and many things can be forgiven, if not forgotten. Women were traditionally brought up to think of themselves as subservient to men, on top of which my mother was a timid woman and obviously nervous of rocking the boat. If she had happiness of her own, and she seems to have done, her attitude was no doubt that she must view the marriage vows seriously as regards taking her husband for better or for worse. For my mother, this must have meant walking an emotional tightrope at times.

The type of man who comes across as a dignified fellow to his colleagues and the outside world, but can display a much less appealing side of his personality in the privacy of his home, is not unheard of. There may be more of them about than we realise. Here is a further observation from my father's former colleague John Shotton: 'It is difficult for me to reconcile the image of the man I knew with the wife beating, the ogre in the house …' That image, of the smartly groomed adjutant with the fine sense of humour, the life and soul of the officers' mess, was Dr Jekyll. By the time he arrived home to my mother, it seems that, despite the fact that he adored her, he sometimes became the frightening

Mr Hyde. Again, what causes this kind of split personality in a man? Did the military experience play a part in affecting my father's behaviour in this way? It's said a soldier's life swings between two extremes – boredom and adrenalin-filled action. In time of war, the boredom may well be outweighed by action, though often with anxious hours of waiting in between. In peacetime though it's the other way around, with endless polishing, marching, parading and inspections, till receiving a posting to one of the world's trouble spots. This is obviously very different from civilian life, where most people, apart from maybe those working in the emergency services, have a relatively consistent daily routine, without sudden, hazardous intervals. Given such circumstances, mood swings wouldn't be that surprising. And for my father's generation, the years following the outbreak of peace in 1945 must have seemed in some ways one long anti-climax. There were various, relatively minor, flashpoints of course, and always the need for vigilance against the Soviet threat from across the Rhine. But once the great struggle against Nazism was won, were soldiers so readily seen as heroes any more? Kipling of course had already identified this fair-weather attitude of the public towards those men who 'guard us while we sleep', in his poem about Tommy Atkins. The contrast between the dramatic days of the war and the 'inactive' decades that came after, when drilling was the norm and action the rarity, may well have hung heavily with my father, hence perhaps the sense of restlessness and frustration that Ian observed in him.

Our father's post-war years were not entirely without incident, however, as I learned from another anecdote told to, and later relayed to me by, his comrade John Shotton. The events concerned took place during one dark winter's night in the early 1960s, at a barracks somewhere in the south of England. Mr Shotton stressed to me that to appreciate the story it is important to understand two things: firstly, the consequences for my father if he had not acted appropriately – i.e. possible court martial, and secondly, the fact that in the army, the word 'double' has two meanings. I will paraphrase Mr Shotton's account as follows. This particular night, my father had been assigned as officer of the guard at his barracks, reporting to the field officer, who remained on duty and on call, at his nearby home. The officer of the guard, the sergeant of the guard and six soldiers comprised the guard, who were all to stay on duty, in uniform, until relieved the following morning. All was quiet that evening until, at around 11pm, there came a news report on the national media, announcing that the IRA had just mounted an attack on a barracks some fifty miles from where my father was stationed, making off with a quantity of arms. The field officer, apparently having heard this report of the attack, either on the TV or radio, urgently called up my father and ordered him to 'double the guard' on the barracks. In this context, to 'double' the guard meant to strengthen it from six to twelve men. Now, as John Shotton points out from his army experience, it is very difficult at 11 o'clock at night to get anyone in the barracks, apart from those actually on guard duty, to do anything, especially after what he calls 'their socialising'. And my father, he says, knew this only too well, and that getting another half-dozen soldiers out at that time of night 'was absolutely impossible' or at least, that 'ordering six tipsy' (in bricklayers' speak: pissed) 'and bolshie men onto a guard at midnight was a liability'. So, bearing in mind that if he failed to carry out his orders he could be court-martialled, what did my father do that night? He decided that, if he couldn't follow the order to double the guard as intended, i.e. by doubling its numbers, he would have to do so in another sense. He therefore went down to the guardroom, hoicked out his sergeant and said 'See those lights at the bottom of the road? What I want is the guard marched down there and back, at the double.' And that is apparently exactly what happened; the men marched down the road at twice the regular speed, allowing my father to report back to the field officer that he'd 'doubled' the guard. John Shotton's comment on this incident is: 'Excellent! [though] some might say to this "God Almighty! Is this what the army is all about?" Well, yes it is. It is demonstrating clarity of thought over stupidity' If the barracks had been attacked, and it had been found there were only six men on guard duty as opposed to twelve as ordered, one wonders how my father's actions would have stood up in an inquiry. It also seems odd to think that military intelligence was supplied courtesy of the 11 o'clock news. It could have been a very serious situation of course, and Mr Shotton does add he has 'no doubt at all that David and the sergeant would then have stayed awake all the night, and indeed put a few hours of sentry duty in themselves. I'm sure about that because it is the sensible thing … and exactly what the David McEwan(s) and my sort do.' The story also has all the makings of an episode of *Dad's Army* – Don't panic Mr Mainwaring! – Fair play to my father though, I suppose, for thinking on his feet, and in fact, Corporal Jones would be running around with a bayonet shouting, 'They don't like it up 'em!' The tactics employed by my father that night sound more like the kind of shrewd stroke Private Walker might have pulled, or perhaps the pedantic Sergeant Wilson. 'Well, you did say "double" the guard sir …'

There have been two Roses in my life. One of them was my mum, the other my mother. If my mum ever felt sad that she and I were not of the same flesh and blood, she had no reason to. She loved me just the same, and I her. The biological part did not matter a jot. Rose McEwan was my flesh and blood, and when I eventually met her, I wondered if she'd ever been sad for the opposite reason – that she hadn't been my mum. Rose McEwan of course had other children, whereas my mum had only me.

A little while after Rose McEwan's funeral, I went back down to the church at Ash. I was going to pay my respects once more, but there was another reason; I wanted to tell Rose something. Entering St Peter's this time I was, apart from two of the friendly parishioners who keep an eye on the place and show visitors around, on my own. How beautifully kept the place was, I thought, noticing the softly gleaming brass-work, the warm sheen of the wooden pews and the pretty arrangements of flowers. A lot of hard work goes into these things and keeping a church spick and span, usually all of it voluntary. The pews at St Peter's are apparently under threat of being replaced by individual chairs, a move the traditionalists are resisting. I can see their point. Apart from the fact the pews are fine pieces of furniture with a rich history, can you imagine fifty-odd chairs all scraping back every time the congregation stands for a hymn? Whether you are religious or not, a church, particularly an old one, usually has a soothing effect on the soul. There is something about the solid, ancient stones, which have witnessed so many births and marriages and deaths, the unending cycles of life, that allows one to think, to get a bit of perspective on things, even dare I say, see the bigger picture. I crossed to the far wall, my feet rattling conspicuously over the iron floor grilles. Gazing up at the stained-glass windows, I studied the scenes depicted in the intricately latticed coloured glass. The first window features Roman legionnaires brandishing swords and spears. The rich blue, purple and gold of the design, the flowing raiment and gleaming weaponry, all heighten the warlike feel. I moved to look at another window, one that shows a mother cradling a baby, whilst two older children stand at her side. Above them, winged angels look down, carrying banners proclaiming 'peace' and 'goodwill'. These contrasting scenes might almost represent two distinct phases of my mother's life. The first window suggested the drama of war and the call to arms that had claimed the life of her young Ernest. The second window could be Rose in the new era of peace, with her new born son Ian in her arms. The children not being held might be Roy and Margaret, connected yet not quite with her. And there was no fourth child in the picture. 'Thou shalt not commit adultery', says one of the Ten Commandments. 'Honour thy father and thy mother' runs another. But there's no mention of parents honouring their children. In the stained-glass window the angels with their messages of peace and goodwill were looking down benignly on the woman. If this vision were Rose, then whatever sins she may have committed, or thought she had done, were here being forgiven.

I strolled out and around the side of the church, taking the narrow footpath that led down into the cemetery. There I stood and gazed at the rows of monuments which stretched out amid the tree-lined paths. The earliest of the graves there were well over a hundred years old. Their weathered stones leaned this way and that, nudged out of true by the slowly shifting earth of many decades, their moss-covered inscriptions long indistinct. No one tended these now. In stark contrast was an area of the cemetery set out for the recent graves of children. Some buried here were no more than babies, others were toddlers or older. A few were for children who had died in their early teens. All were very well tended. There were poems and messages of love from parents, brothers and sisters, grandparents, favourite toys and football team emblems placed carefully next to the shining marble headstones. It must be a terrible thing to see your child die, long before your own natural time has come. And how precious and at the same time tenuous our lives are. Illness or accident can so cruelly snatch any of us away, at any time.

I crossed up towards the rear of the Ash Museum, which backs onto the cemetery. I skirted the building, and walked down the broad path leading from the main road. Along this path, set at an angle on a low wall, is a line of memorials of deceased who have been cremated. Above where these people's ashes have been laid, are fixed small, plain nameplates. I stopped by one and read the inscription: 'Rose McEwan 24.09.1915 – 26.12.2003, Remembered With Love By Her Family'. There is nothing ostentatious about that. Name, rank and number, you could say, and no pack drill. Officer David McEwan might even approve, although the word love is included. His own ashes remained, I had been told, unscattered, filed away in a corporation storeroom somewhere.

The former soldier Mr Shotton, who contacted Ian with memories of his colleague, our father, had been intrigued by the fact my mother had surrendered not only me, but to all intents and purposes her first two offspring as well. He wrote: 'Regarding 1948 and the giving away of two further children, would this have affected Rose's personality?' It's a good question; how did the giving away of me, and then later being apart from her first two children, affect my mother? Mr Shotton had no definite answers, but did refer to other cases known personally to him where mothers had left their families to run off with better-placed men. His only conclusion is that such examples beg the general question of whether 'women are not the tigresses we always thought they were when it comes to their cubs?' Rose may have abandoned one or more of her 'cubs' but did she forget them? The first two she stayed in contact with, and was, I believe, later on especially close to Margaret, more so than Ian, but what of the third? That first birthday card to Spring Terrace suggests that, for a while at least, she didn't forget me. But what of later – did time eventually heal the wound, fill whatever painful void my enforced wrenching away had left in her heart? As the years passed, had I even entered her thoughts? Could this painful question ever be answered?

Ian had already told me how, thinking back to events in the mid 1950s, when our parents had attempted to adopt a brother for him, he thought it possible that our mother had all along been wanting to come and search for me, to retrace her fateful journey to Reading Station that winter of 1942, to try to reclaim the child she had, with such anguish, such heart-wrenching pain, surrendered. And what greater anguish may, or must, surely have followed as the years ticked by, watching Ian grow up a solitary child, while her other little boy, Ian's brother, grew up in the arms of strangers. How my mother must have ached with remorse, longed to go back in time, wracked with despair to undo what she had done and begging her husband to go and search for me and return me to her arms. Was this really how it had been for my mother – enduring pain, a searing sense of loss? Her ill-fated attempt to adopt another little boy, a fair-haired substitute for me, is surely evidence of her regret at what had happened.

Thinking about how the events in this drama were destined to unfold after 1942, one sees, perhaps, if it wasn't already apparent, with a sense of shock, that there is a piercingly tragic irony to the story. I will come to this in a moment. First, consider my mother's state of mind back in November 1942 and during the period shortly afterwards. Having abandoned me to strangers that day on the station, and disappeared back to her own life, what were her plans and expectations, her mood and feelings in the months that followed? What indeed was the subsequent state of affairs between her and my father? Did they continue their illicit liaison, clutching, like so many people during those dark days of the war, at what pleasure and companionship they could, living each day as if it might be their last till the Nazis bombed us into oblivion or drove their Panzers into our towns and villages? In 1942 there was little light on the horizon for our beleaguered island, and despite the mood of defiance, few dared to imagine the more ominous future that might well be in store for themselves and their families. As the air raid sirens wailed, did my mother and father try like everyone else to forget their anxieties in a drink, a singsong and the comforts of bed? In the months after November 1942, my mother, even in her worst moments of anguish at the enforced surrender of her child, may have consoled herself with the knowledge that it had been exactly that – an action that had no alternative. 'I just had to', as she had repeated over and over to her sister, my Auntie Margaret, on the sad journey away from Reading Station after leaving me on the platform. But think about this: the words 'I had to' may have been a consolation for my mother at the time of the deed, simply because, the probabilities of wartime aside, she expected her husband Ernest back. But things were to look very different a few months later. Shortly after D-Day, having sustained injuries in action at Nijmegen, Ernest passed away in hospital. The moment my mother learned of his death, the overwhelming necessity for having abandoned me no longer applied. If ever there was a desire to turn back the clock, it must have been the moment she received that telegram. Now it's true that, if Ernest had already been dead when I was born, my father, fearing implications for his career, and for other reasons, may still have argued for my disposal; but the overriding motive at the time must surely have been the existence of Ernest Wort, away fighting for his country, and the fact that a fellow soldier, a promising candidate for promotion, had committed adultery with that other soldier's wife and got her pregnant. If, in November 1942, my mother could have foreseen her husband's death, how different might the situation and my own subsequent fate have been? And when, in 1944, she was informed of Ernest's death, imagine how she must have felt, any normal grief for her husband and their imperfect relationship completely swallowed up by the appalling realisation that she need not have given away her baby. To be made so brutally aware of this must have cut her like a knife. By this time I was two years old; the previous year my mother had sent me a first birthday card, so I was undoubtedly in her thoughts. With the death of her husband, my mother became free to marry my father. But the very event that liberated her surely brought with it torment. Behind the joyful prospect of a new life with Sergeant Major McEwan stood a dark shadow – the knowledge that the child they had created might, but for a cruel twist of fate, still be in her arms. For my mother, the complete surrender was far from complete. If only, if only, if only, she must have thought to herself, again and again. But alas it was too late. Or was it? Had her deed really been so irrevocable? Perhaps, in my mother's heart there had arisen after Ernest's death and her subsequent shock, a faint glimmer of hope, searching for a chance to go back, to rewind the chain of events that had led her to Reading Station on that cold, December day in 1942. It had seemed unthinkable to desert her child, yet she had done it; why might she not now reverse the procedure and take her child back? There had been nothing official about the infant's handover, and the legal position of its 'adoption' was surely an ambiguous one. She must at least have mulled over what grounds there were, and to whom she could appeal, if she were to ask for her little son to be returned to her? He was after all, living with strangers, only a few miles from her home, learning to walk and talk, with her not knowing whether he was happy or sad, and unable even to see him, let alone hold and comfort him. Given these circumstances, it would seem surprising if, from the moment she learnt of her husband's death, my mother had not been gripped by a burning desire to take me back.

But had she thought of me since? More recently, my brother Ian had told me something else. And the thing he had told me was what had prompted me to return to the little church at Ash. I now wanted to speak to Rose. I had something to tell her. It stemmed from a particular visit Ian had made to our mother while she was in the nursing home. On his way out, one of Rose's carers had told him that she and Rose had recently been chatting casually about someone who had had a miscarriage. Quite unprompted, Rose had remarked that she too had once 'lost a child'. Through the fog of time, she had remembered something. I unwrapped the bunch of white tulips I had brought with me and arranged them carefully above Rose's resting place. For the second time in my life I had brought my mother flowers. I was never lost, only mislaid.

POSTSCRIPT

The past they say is another country. If so then the first months of our lives are a country from which we are banished; at least, directly so. After all, who can consciously remember much about being a baby? No sooner have we entered the world than a door closes behind us. Memory's a funny thing, often deceptive and unreliable. Some of our earliest childhood recollections may have been planted in our heads — by relations and acquaintances recounting events and fond anecdotes, usually half-remembered ones, consciously or unconsciously embroidering and adjusting them in an endless game of Chinese whispers. Other people's imperfect memories can sometimes become our own, though if we're fortunate we'll find someone who, sooner or later, will talk to us about the very early part of our life and tell it like it was.

As we grow, our own memory kicks in and starts to

record things. But it also starts to pick and choose. As we remember we also forget. If everything that happened to us stayed at the front of our minds we'd probably go insane, and 'what's too painful to remember we simply choose to forget', as the song goes. Freud, the granddaddy of trick-cyclists, would disagree, claiming that nothing is ever really forgotten, only stored in the unconscious. I've often wondered where the unconscious is. The basement of a tall building perhaps, where in some neglected corner of an office dusty old files are stacked up, waiting to be sorted out some day. 'The Numbskulls' might have pictured it like that in their weekly cartoon strip in the *Dandy*, or was it the *Beano*? I forget now. Better check my unconscious.

It's not only memories that get pushed away; sometimes human beings must be relocated too. When I was a lad millions of people were 'disappearing' under the smiling gaze of Mao and Stalin. Of course we knew nothing about it at the time. Everyone knows history gets deliberately, secretly rewritten, and the same thing can happen in families, for good, bad or indifferent reasons. At the age of fifteen I found out it had happened in my own family, to me. But although I was aware from then on that my life had not started out as I'd always previously assumed, it was to be decades before I uncovered the true story and learned where I actually came from. But whatever gaps and distortions may occur over time, whether in our national history or that of our selves and our families, facts will always be facts and truth, truth. The events of years gone by do not alter, although they are frequently hidden from us, waiting to be uncovered, dusted down and calmly examined. However much water flows under the bridge of time, that bridge may still be found, providing us with a stepping stone to the past, a return journey to the truth.

There was never any real question mark about the precise time I was born. It was November 1942, and when I first opened my eyes on the world much of Europe was ablaze with violence. Behind brave faces fear and uncertainty gripped the hearts of millions of ordinary people. Britain, summoning up the bulldog spirit, was on a 'sticky wicket', despite Roosevelt's pledge to be the arsenal of democracy after the attack on Pearl Harbour. The Battle of Britain had already been fought in the skies over Kent two years previously and won at great cost to our flying boys. Paris and most of France had fallen to the Nazis and now only the English Channel lay between them and us. In January 1942 Pathe News showed the shock footage of what was described as 'Hitler's yellow brothers launching a cowardly attack on our island fortress of Singapore'. The Empire was under siege and so were we, not only from conventional bombing. On 4 November, a few days before I was born, the first V1 rocket was dropped, a weapon that was to strike terror into civilians, especially in London and other cities targeted by the Luftwaffe. If I'd been a nine- or ten-year-old at the time I'd doubtless have been scared, but like a lot of kids would also have seen the war as a bit of an adventure –

out collecting shrapnel, plane spotting, singing 'Hitler is a twerp', that sort of thing. It depended on where you were, I suppose. The cockneys knew all about it during the worst months of the blitz, and when a bomb did fall on Buckingham Palace, the Queen, our late Queen Mother, expressed relief she could now 'face the East-enders'. I'm sure you know all this, and anyone can look in a history book for facts. Truth is another matter, and as someone once said, it's rarely pure and never simple.

Of course ordinary life continued during the war, and people ate, slept, worked, gossiped, got drunk, told lies, made money, love and promises, some of which were kept. They say a nation at war is at peace with itself, all in the same boat and all that. For many people the war was the time they felt most alive. Some even remember the air raids as exciting, dangerous, yes, but the darkness and urgency were a bit of a thrill too, especially when no one knew for certain how long they might be around in this world to enjoy themselves. Casual sex didn't begin in the 1960s.

To the residents of Binfield Heath, the village in rural Oxfordshire in which I grew up, there may have been less bombing, but most people would have had relatives or friends fighting overseas. And those on the home front would usually be engaged in the war effort in some way. The Henbest family for example had four sons serving their country and a daughter doing war work in a factory. Mr Henbest, a veteran of the First World War was in 'Dad's Army', the village home guard. I have a little local history book that mentions them and paints a vivid picture of our community at the time. The author of the book records that his two nephews were lost in action. Many of the other people in the book I came to know as I grew up in the area – all of the six lads playing a really serious-looking game of conkers, for example. The scenery depicted in the black and white 1940s' photographs is little altered today, including Lord Phillimore's two thousand-acre estate, which provided me with useful employment as a lad, working as a beater during the shooting season. That was still the age of deference, just. Doffing your cap to the gentry and the notion of 'God bless the squire and all his relations and keep us in our proper stations' might have fallen off a bit, but there were still clear boundaries between them and us. Where the boundaries are nowadays is harder to see. Maybe the years of my youth were still the good old days or maybe not. Rose-tinted spectacles notwithstanding, a lot of the respect that people back then had for one another has withered, definitely. In the 1950s those that didn't know about respect soon learned it. The village coppers knew who the bad apples were, and could also tell the difference between a thug and a lad who was just simple, avoiding the kind of wealth-creation schemes for lawyers and bureaucrats that exist today. The police were unafraid to do their job and people did feel more secure; it's not just a dewy-eyed myth. Maybe we can have that world again.

Binfield Heath was and still is in many ways idyllic. It's certainly picturesque, and the kind of place that people who haven't visited these shores may imagine all English people reside in. And my home today is only a few minutes' drive from those green fields of my boyhood. I've lived in south Oxfordshire all of my life, well all but six weeks of it, and if your idea of England is something out of *Midsomer Murders* then you won't be disappointed round here, or surprised to learn that several episodes of the programme have been filmed in the area. Many of the local residents have appeared as extras while Inspector Barnaby racked his brains over the latest juicy corpse found in the deep freeze or collapsed at the village fete. In reality we don't have many murders in this part of England, but our cricket green, half-timbered pubs and warm beer are all authentic, and we even have amateur dramatics. I was brought up a country boy and have been happy to remain one, content not to stray far from my roots. And growing up in a traditional tranquil rural community, a place of fresh air and open space, with the war over before I knew anything about it and free milk and medical care on its way, my well-being was hardly an outside chance. Far more important though was the fact, taken joyfully for granted, that my world had two wonderful people in it. I knew that they cared for me without question, and for as long as I could remember had wrapped me in the cocoon of their love. They were my parents Rose and Percy Sharp. This book is intended as a celebration of them, of finding my birth relatives after so many years, and as a unique piece of family history.

This book started out as nothing more than bits and

pieces of writing that would tell my grandsons a little about my life. Nobody's life runs in a straight line and for me, at times, it has been an exceptional and emotional journey. My hope is that in thirty, maybe forty, years time, when I am long gone and my grandsons are grown up with homes and families of their own and this book is long forgotten and gathering dust in some dark corner, they may discover it once again and, having read it, smile and say, 'yes, that was my granddad.'

Daylight delights you,
Love just follows you.
Our hearts rejoice.
God in all his glory,
take care of you.

Written by Rose McEwan, my mother, shortly before she died.